International
Cinema
{ A User's Manual }

ROBERT A. JORDAN

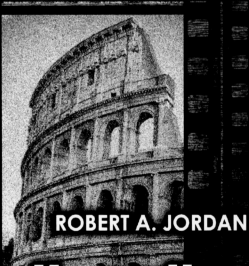

Kendall Hunt
publishing company

Kendall Hunt
publishing company

www.kendallhunt.com
Send all inquiries to:
4050 Westmark Drive
Dubuque, IA 52004-1840

Printed in the United States of America

Dedication

For Michael

Wherever You Are

Contents

Acknowledgments

The acknowledgments page of a text book will most likely mention folks who aided the author in writing that book: academic associates, experts in the field, even the guy who answered an obscure question sent by e-mail – though they've never even met.

I believe in something more basic. In fact, you could probably call it one of my core principles or something like that. You and I are "whole people." Each part of our lives influences all the other parts. If you have broken your leg, it affects your whole life. Your ability to work will be impacted. Your emotional life may be filled with frustration. Your relationship with friends and family will suffer. And that's "just" a broken leg. If you suffer from severe, clinical depression, you might withdraw from everyone you know. You might be unable to sleep. A painful divorce—you get the idea. All parts of your life influence your whole life. Good or bad.

Writing a book isn't something done in a vacuum. It's part of that whole person too. So it isn't just an academic colleague who helps to get it written. That dear friend who you can call on to meet you for coffee in the lonely hours of the night is an essential part of getting that book written, even if they don't know it.

For me, I've had a brain tumor. It was removed successfully, but has left me with a number of types of damage that I won't get into here. More than just writing this book, I literally wouldn't make it through if not for loving, supportive family, and friends.

So there are two groups of people I need to acknowledge here. First, I do want to thank just a few of the people who helped me write this book—film experts who have influenced my own work, especially the wonderful professors who have shared their love of this subject with me.

I wish to recognize the work of author and film historian, David Cook; the fascinating words of Leonard Maltin and Roger Ebert. While I have not seen him in many years, I will always value and admire Kevin Brownlow—a person I will always consider to be my friend.

Three film professors have especially inspired me. David Shepard. Drew Casper. Rick Jewell. Gentlemen, it's been a long time, but you are each greatly appreciated.

But I also want to thank that second group of people. The family and friends who have been there for me through the tough times. My wife, Robyn, and other members of my family have done more than I can say. And I am also blessed with friends who have encouraged me through this process. La Shawn Rivers gets to hear me vent when things are bad. My personal four horsemen, Victoria, Kathryn, Joe and Emily – make me smile (which doesn't happen too often anymore)—and sometimes we even talk about cinema. Old friends Ken Fields and Chuck Strickland always seem to know just when I need someone to take me to lunch. And Alexie Price—I miss our conversations.

Introduction

My goal for this book is based on an imaginary conversation. No, it's not as crazy as it sounds. In this conversation, a film fan, maybe even a college film student, is chatting with a person in the world of film—it might be a studio employee, or a critic, or a professor. Maybe even a well-known director. I'll just call the first of these people "You" and the other person I'll call "Joss," for no reason.

After exchanging pleasantries, you ask "Joss," "So what sort of films are you really most interested in?"

"Oh man," he answers, lighting up. "Everyone is so addicted to big American action films—super heroes and stuff. That's great and all, but I am really going in a different direction. I'm so hooked on old European classics, ya know?"

"Yeah, sure."

"I think I've seen *Children of Paradise* about a dozen times. I think I'd erase every film I've ever made, if I could say I made *that*!"

"Really?"

"I guess most people don't expect it of me. I just love stuff like *The Grand Illusion* or *The Rules of the Game*. I'm just glad I can talk to someone who can relate!"

"Um, yeah, *Rules of the Game*."

"*Metropolis*." He begins to look at you strangely.

"*Metropolis* didn't really do that much for me." You are beginning to feel like an unarmed person in a battle of wits.

Joss or whatever his name is, isn't grinning any longer. "You haven't seen any of those films, have you." It isn't a question.

"Actually, no."

"I thought you had studied film."

"I have! I've seen everything Martin Scorsese has ever done!"

"Go get me a coffee."

———

My point (and I do have one) is that there is a very basic level of viewing experience that I will call **cinemaliteracy**, which will be assumed. If a film person, like that described above knows you have even a passing experience with cinema, they will assume you have at least seen these films. Yes, their personal favorite film may be *Oldboy*, but they understand if you have never seen it. But *The Cabinet of Dr. Caigari*? Honestly, for any person who claims to be a student of film (in school, self-taught, whatever), but has not seen *that*, is the equivalent of someone claiming to be a literature major or being well-read not knowing the name Charles Dickins. *That is a fail.*

There are thousands of international films out there and more every year. I recently looked at a very exhaustive and authoritative film text book and counted references to over ten thousand film titles. Even if you were attempting to see all the "important" international films, once you had decided just what made a particular film important, you'd still be watching over one hundred films easily. While doing so might actually be fun, clearly, to approach even a "basic level," a "core," we will have to cut even deeper.

So my goal here is to just offer a basic level of cinemaliteracy. That means starting off with the essentials. And that's what this book will do. In almost every case, each film studied is simply essential.[1] A masterwork that it will be assumed you have seen and even studied to a reasonable degree. We will start small, but the films in this text are a must.

Clearly, one of the most important and difficult things that I had to do is to cut. I had to eliminate entire types of film, just to be left with a workable body of films. Sad, but necessary. This book will essentially ignore all documentary (non-fiction) films. There will be no real analysis of experimental, avant-garde cinema. Animated films had to be eliminated (sorry *anime* lovers). As an apology, let me just say that I believe what is left will absolutely amaze you.

So that's what the book *doesn't* do. What *does* it do?

I will provide a necessary first look at a group of films that are absolutely essential viewing for anyone seriously interested in cinema. Furthermore, in most cases, I will offer an analysis of the critical cinema movements these films represent. The essays, on film or movement, will be brief and easy to read, but give you an extremely large amount of information to serve as your foundation. I write in an easy, casual style (which you probably already know by now) and my goal is to make it a "pleasant read" for you. I refuse to include shot-by-shot recreations of films. I can (and have) open a text book to find 17 pages of nothing but pictures detailing "The Odessa Steps" sequence of *The Battleship Potemkin*. It is my opinion that in the 21st century, someone interested in examining each and every shot in a film has the ability to get a DVD and watch it as much as they want. In many cases, they can even find it on the Internet. If I really want to have students in my class examine the shot selection that closely in class, I can provide a lecture presentation that shows each image for them. I do not see the need for you to pay for 17 pages of solid "Odessa Steps" photos.

A word of caution: Just because I make a joke or you find my discussion of a particular film to be unconventional, do not make the mistake of assuming that the book is silly and that you don't need to look for serious information. It's a bit of a tightrope. If I write a book in a serious, heavy academic tone, the reader knows it's serious, but falls asleep. If I write a book in a casual style and even get sarcastic from time to time, the reader doesn't mind the reading nearly so much, but figures that it must not be important if the author seems to make light of it at times. There are HUGE issues confronted in these films: the nature of war, what divides nations and religions one from another, how guilt can utterly destroy not just an individual's soul, but those of everyone around him in the process. What is the nature of Man's relationship to God? If I crack a sarcastic joke about the director, or something like that, do not assume I am not taking the subject matter seriously—or that you shouldn't.

---

1 Okay, *The Official Story* and *Moolaadé* are not strictly speaking, "essential," but they represent something essential about international film. And *3 Idiots*? Well, it's just an exceptional film that happens to make my heart happy, so I wrote about it—so there!

A final word on the "Give Me Your Feedback" pages. If you are a classroom student using this as a textbook, there are two ways to complete the worksheets (at least two). Some students will answer the questions two minutes before turning it in and do so by using the fewest possible number of words. Others will think about the questions carefully. List items that they remember from the film and thought were important. Give *their* opinions, not what someone else might think. If using these worksheets applies to you, ask yourself, *what do you suppose exam questions are based upon?*

So anyway, a quick, easy read. Mountains of information that will make the films you screen much more meaningful (and to be easy to access if there is a test). Written to be an essential foundation—a starting point. Use it. Make it work for you. That's why I wrote it.

ORIGINS OF CINEMA

PRE-CINEMA

Writing about beginnings is difficult. You might be able to identify the specific day an event took place, but then you think about all the important incidents that lead up to it. Or you identify the key people who are major players in the story, but just as quickly, you see how many others influenced them in unexpected ways. In some cases, you won't even be able to determine exactly when something took place. If the event is ancient, there might even be a whole set of legends about it—and maybe none of them are accurate!

Here we are going to examine international cinema. Many of the films we can see for ourselves, even today. Many of the major personalities' lives have been well-documented. But when it comes to the origins, there are some "wild cards" in the mix. Just what event do we identify as the "dawn of film?" What machine do we even call "the very first motion picture camera?" Is there a definite first-showing of a moving picture to a public audience?

To make matters worse, when you read any detailed history about cinema, you quickly realize that there are many truly ancient machines that are clearly related to the cameras and projectors we will come to know. There are even children's toys that use basic optical principles to give the illusion of motion, clear back in Rome and Greece.

Where we really have to begin in even a brief survey of the origins of cinema is not with an event or a machine. We begin with the human body itself. The eye has abilities, characteristics, which give us the possibility of someday seeing motion pictures.

The human brain understands and interprets images in certain ways that will someday make it possible for us to watch cinema.

So we begin with a bit of basic human physiology. When the eye sees an image flash before it and disappear, that image is retained for a fraction of a second. It's called **Persistence of Vision**. When it receives images, the human brain interprets those overlapping and slightly changing images as if they were moving. This brain interpretation is called **The Phi Phenomena**. So without getting too technical, the way our eyes see the rapidly flickering still images of a film and the way our brains interpret these images as if they are moving—together these human traits prepared us to see movies all the way back to the dawn of humanity!

Whew! That was as biological and physiological as we need to get, thankfully. Suffice to say, even crude toys and experiments can cause us to see the illusion of movement: quick flip cards with a dancing cartoon figure printed on them, a fan with a bird printed on one side and a cage on the other, which you are intended to spin. In the 19th Century, sequential photographs of someone running. They are like hints at what is to come.

One "pre-cinema" endeavor is worth our attention here. In 1872, a photographer named **Eadweard Muybridge** was hired to settle a bet: when at a gallop, do all four of a horse's hooves leave the ground simultaneously? Since humans could not see this for themselves, Muybridge came up with the cleaver idea of mounting 12 cameras around a track and having them shoot an image set off by the horse hitting a tripwire. For the record, the horse does indeed come completely off the ground at one phase of gallop. More importantly, the various still photos recorded the horse's motion in a way humans had never seen before. Muybridge called it **series photography**. Flashing quickly from one image to the next, we are essentially seeing a moving picture of the horse.

TRUE MOTION PICTURES: TWO VERSIONS

The 19th Century was a time of amazing invention: the telephone was invented in 1875, the phonograph in 1877 and the electric light bulb in 1879, to name only a few. It was only a matter of time until the great inventors of the era turned their attention to photography.

There were several important moving picture machine inventors, and others who contributed critical pieces of the puzzle, like the sprocket holes set at the side of the film strip. Without them, a piece of film quickly slid out of place and movies couldn't be even a minute long!

I want to limit our discussion here to just two cinema projects—one in America and one in France.[2] In America, the name most often associated with the motion picture is the legendary inventor, **Thomas Edison**. Ironically, Edison didn't see much potential for the moving picture. He primarily wanted a visual recording element to add to his audio recording phonograph. Truly, in 1893 his assistant, **W. K. L. Dickson** is the one who actually invented what history would remember as Edison's motion picture. You may never hear the name of the man again, but here, at least, let us honor Mr. Dickson.

The Edison (Dickson) machine may have come early in the race, but it was far from without weaknesses. The camera was set semi-permanently inside a small building (with a glass roof to let in sunlight). *The subject had to come to the camera in order to be photographed!* Most of the surviving Edison films show a subject performing on a stage. This may not seem like a big deal, but think of cinema's ability to capture events and objects in the real world. The Edison machine could not go out there to see them!

Another film machine came in 1895 from the **Lumiere brothers** of France.[3] While obviously not the winner of the race, the Lumiere machine had several features that made it truly fascinating. It was small, perhaps the size of a large briefcase, by today's standards. You could carry it with you anywhere. There are surviving Lumiere films shot everywhere from the local zoo to the remote location of a war. In addition, the machine was, what we would call, multipurpose. It could photograph objects as a camera, but you could disassemble it and develop your film in it. Then you could put a light source inside and use it to project your films on a wall or screen. It was portable and it was a camera, developing kit and projector all in one! By the turn of the century, Lumiere cameramen were traveling around the globe with this light and versatile equipment and we can still see many of the resulting films today. Trains arriving at the station, royalty on parade, presidents in their own homes, even the great San Francisco earthquake and fire—a cameraman happened to be right there!

THE BIRTH OF THE STORY FILM

It is easy to see how inventors would become interested in motion photography and their work would obviously lead to experiments, improvements and displays to the public. But just what was the appeal to the rest of us? Honestly, in those early years of motion pictures, the audiences were simply fascinated with the movement itself. It may be difficult for us to appreciate today, but at that time, this was the *first time* anyone had seen a ship sailing across the bay, animals frolicking at the zoo, a far-off site like the Statue of Liberty. It was a novelty—a *fad*. But in your experience, how long do fads last? This year's Christmas obsession might be in the clearance bin already next year! Fads are short. Even in the early 20th Century, most people had probably seen a moving picture show once or twice—and it *wasn't* something you'd want to go back to dozens of times! If moving subjects were all cinema could offer, the fad would run its course and die out within just a few years.

Fortunately, film took a significant leap. Once films could run longer without fouling the projector, filmmakers began telling STORIES. As early as 1902 you can begin seeing very interesting productions,

---

[2] There was an even earlier motion picture machine developed by Louis Le Prince in 1887. However, he is not well known today. We will focus on the efforts of Edison and Lumiere. Unfair? Absolutely!

[3] The brothers' names were Louis and Auguste, but you don't need to remember their first names on my account!

An iconic image from the Méliès film *A Trip to the Moon* (1902). When watching any of his films, we are constantly aware that this man was a magician!

including *The Life of an American Fireman* (US) and *A Trip to the Moon* (France). The latter film introduces us to one of the very first film masters, a magician named **Georges Méliès**. Try to appreciate the difference here. Edison was an inventor. The Lumieres were inventors. This man was an *entertainer*. Méliès made films that were an extension of his magic act. They are fascinating. *They entertain.* Gone are the days of seeing a train pulling into a station. A Méliès film tells a little story. It flaunts a wonderful camera trick. Even today, when you see a film by him, you will still be amazed at Méliès' care and his creativity. If the Lumieres showed the real world as it is, Méliès showed us fantasy. He gave us subjective imagination—the *unreal*, if you will.

George Méliès was the leading filmmaker, at least in Europe until about 1907. But by then the once fresh and original magician was behind the times and repeating old formulas. Well before World War I, he had been overtaken by major businesses and had essentially been forgotten.[4]

THE EMPIRE OF PATHÉ

In 1896, Charles Pathé began a film company that would become the largest in the world by about 1905 and would continue to dominate, especially in Europe, until the start of World War I. MGM, Paramount, Universal—we are familiar with the

American studios, but Pathé was actually larger than any of them. Before World War I, France (and perhaps surprisingly Italy) were just as influential as America in the global film world. A ruthless businessman, Pathé has sometimes been called "the Napoleon of Cinema." Roughly 60 percent of the films made in this era were produced by Pathé. The company even manufactured its own film stock.

This sort of dominance was short-lived. World War I changed everything.

WORLD WAR I AND THE DOMINANCE OF HOLLYWOOD

When the war hit Europe, the result for the world of cinema was inevitable. Imagine your business was dominated by just two companies, one with facilities in the south and one in the north. Then imagine that an absolutely massive storm hits the southern region. It wipes out the southern company utterly. All its manufacturing facilities are leveled. Many of its employees are left homeless. Some of its key personnel are even killed! Meanwhile, the northern company faces a few minor inconveniences, such as a raise in taxes or rationing. But they are virtually untouched. They continue business as usual. The southern company? They might even go out of business. But assuming they do try to put the pieces back together, they will be perhaps 20 years behind their rival.

There are other reasons why Hollywood film production became more popular in this era, but I think the World War is the critical element. While Pathé experienced a literal war, Hollywood came through relatively unscathed and continued film production at a much more advanced level than any other national cinema in the world. It is a lead they kept for decades and the name Hollywood has been synonymous with motion pictures ever since.[5]

THE HOLLYWOOD STANDARD

When it came to making film an entertainment form that the whole world would crave, Hollywood was simply remarkable. Hollywood stars were known all over the globe and the films of the late silent era were a "universal language" of sorts that could be

---

[4] By the 1920s, his filmmaking abandoned, Méliès could be found in a shop at a railway station. The book, *The Invention of Hugo Cabret* and the resulting film, *Hugo*, are loose tales of his later life.

[5] By no means do I intend to downplay the heroic war efforts of Americans like directors William Wellman, Merian C. Cooper, and actors George O'Brien and Randolph Scott.

American Cinema. The primary way films were understood early in the silent era was as entertainment. Hollywood story films became the most successful films of the era—and they are what we are most familiar with today. But other kinds of film were possible, especially in other parts of the world. Here four early film giants join together to found United Artists Studio: Douglas Fairbanks, Sr., Mary Pickford, Charlie Chaplin, and legendary director D. W. Griffith.

marketed in multiple countries, with no concern over language. Charlie Chaplin had nicknames in a variety of different countries. Silent stars Mary Pickford and Douglas Fairbanks went to London for their honeymoon, so they would not be bothered by their American fans, but were shocked when they were mobbed in both London and Paris.

The exciting film stories. Endearing characters. The world loved Hollywood movies and their recipe became the standard for entertainment films all over the world. This book deliberately avoids discussing American cinema at length, but it is critical to acknowledge that it is Hollywood story films that will be the norm—the standard—by which we compare and contrast the variety of international films that we are about to examine. Films from other countries may attempt to mimic Hollywood, or they may go in radically different directions, but I still think it is useful to consider the American entertainment form as a starting point and as a useful comparison.

FILM AS NIGHTMARE: GERMAN EXPRESSIONISM

The German Weimar Republic must have seemed to start with such promise. World War I was over and the seeds of a new social era could be seen in many parts of Germany. But what will be remembered forever when one mentions the Weimar Republic is inflation, chaos and the ushering in of the Nazi era.

To simplify the story, money caused much of the problem in the Post-WWI Republic. Barely able to keep above water financially, Germany was suddenly faced with a catastrophic bill: in the Versailles Treaty, Germany was essentially charged for the war. There was not enough money in all of Germany to pay for the astronomical fees demanded! When the German government printed more money, the value of their mark plummeted. After the war, the mark was worth roughly seven marks to the dollar. By 1921 it was worth only 330 marks to the dollar. Within two years, it would take 4.2 *billion* marks to buy a single dollar. By this time, workers would bring wheelbarrows to work to get their wages and once they got home, it wasn't worth enough to buy groceries!

Try to imagine this sort of hyper-inflation. It would affect every aspect of life, including the films of the era. The stamp you purchased for postage today would not be sufficient tomorrow. In fact, the post office would run out of stamp designs and be unable to keep up with the printing of new denominations. So old stamps were recycled: a stamp labeled 25 marks, for example, would simply have a line printed across it, deleting the 25 mark price and a second amount would be printed over it, such as 50,000 marks.

Imagine that you and I happened to see each other in a grocery store one day. If we stopped and talked about a great movie you just saw, the price for the can of beans in your hand may have gone up—just during the time we stood chatting.

Money was worth so little in those days that many Germans actually used their mark bills as wallpaper.

If your money was worth nothing, would you go to work? How would you pay your rent? If the current government seemed impotent to fix the crisis, just how far would you go to put a government in place that seemed likely to do something?

Films of this era were of three basic types. The first were what I will call historical epics. These grand period pieces boasted well-known subject matter, such as *Anna Boleyn* (1920), the story of King Henry VIII and his wife (directed by legendary filmmaker Ernst Lubitsch). Big budgets, fine sets, and costumes. An appropriate descriptive word might be "lavish."

An example of the historical epic in Germany during the Weimar era. *Anna Boleyn* (1920) features a grand story, sets, and costumes.

Paramount Pictures/Photofest

The second type of film common in this era was, well, porn. Yes, you heard me correctly (and now you will be sure to get that question correct on your exam). Pornographic films were common in Weimar Germany and indeed flooded the film markets of Europe. And if you care, *this was bad porn*.[6] The films were "disguised" as educational films (*venereal disease in Berlin*) or as documentaries (*the life of a prostitute*). Yes, these were real junk. And they were also one of the most common types of cinema in the German silent era. We just won't be studying them.

The third type of film in this era was expressionistic. The **German expressionist films** accounted only for roughly 10 percent of cinema in the era, but it is these films that have captured the attention of film fans and students ever since.

There are two elements of expressionist films that are equally important to remember. First, these films have a most striking visual quality. They are some of the most strange-looking films ever. The words that will come to mind include, eerie, shadowy, sinister, twisted, and disturbing. If you see examples of the best-known expressionist films, examine the way they look. When you see these (and other) films yourself, the *look* of the films will grab your attention immediately. This isn't just something you'll see in *The Cabinet of Dr. Caligari*. Over and over you'll see images that remind you of nightmares. The F. W. Murnau film *Nosferatu* (1922) stars an actor who is still recognized today as one of the most horrific vampires in cinema. Another lesser-known film by Murnau is *Faust* (1926). The protagonist calls up Satan at a lonely crossroads. *Waxworks* (1924) features dark and ominous images of evil characters like Ivan the Terrible and Jack the Ripper. To say these films are dark and shadowy is simply not enough. The expressionists' intent—their very goal—was to disturb the audience. They wanted you to leave the theater feeling doomed, paranoid—yes, even just a little freaked.

The second element of the expressionist recipe is the fatalistic subject matter. Words will come to your mind such as "doomed" "occult" "paranoid" and even "Satanic." These are stories about death, nightmares, insanity, and evil. It is important to consider the subject matter of these films in the context of the social chaos and hopelessness of Weimar Germany. A film portraying a man who sells his soul or the story of someone who has a good side and an evil side as well make perfect sense in that context. One film from the movement is best-known today as *Destiny* (1921), but its original German title is *The Weary Death*. In this Fritz Lang film, Death is a character and is indeed tired of his work and wants to find his own escape.

There are a dozen expressionist films that could be used as examples. Three top the list for viewers new to the movement. *The Cabinet of Dr. Caligari* is absolutely essential. It is arguably one of the top 10 most-recognized masterworks in film history. Mentioned above, *Nosferatu* is one of the first great vampire movies and continues to fascinate and inspire today. The third film's inclusion in the expressionist movement is debatable. *Metropolis* is a science fiction classic and, again, an essential film to see. Some authorities would argue that it isn't strictly an expressionist film. I'd suggest that it still has some of the most interesting visual design elements of the era and offers plenty of the dark, eerie, and hallucinatory material so common in these films.

These are the masterworks of the movement. If they interest you, there are a handful of others that can be suggested as a "next step" of sorts. There are also important contributions to German silent cinema after expressionism, which are worth our attention as well. German silent film is a truly rich site and it is rife with unusual and surprising gems for any film fan, regardless of your experience level.

---

[6] *Please* don't ask me to give you any examples of *good* silent pornography.

THE FIRST ZOMBIE FILM: THE CABINET OF DR. CALIGARI (1920)

The Cabinet of Dr. Caligari is arguably the best-known film of the German expressionist movement and it is clearly one of the most important international films for any student of cinema to examine. Without question, this is a film you will *not* understand or be able to discuss *without* having seen it yourself, trust me. Assuming you have watched it, let's examine some of the significant facets of the film.

First, the obvious: you will notice the strange and distorted visual design of the film right from the start. There are no right angles. No sets that make the spectator feel comfortable and welcome. The film, well, it just isn't *right*. Not only is this deliberate; it is essential. The movie is the story of a nightmare—perhaps even the ravings of a lunatic. That is the essential nature of *Caligari* and the film expresses it visually. In the modern era, you may find the film story to be clichéd or even corny, but even more than 90 years later, you will still find the visual design to be unsettling, eerie, threatening. Just as the filmmakers intended so long ago.

Examine just one scene: the abduction of the girl, Jane, by the killer, Cesare. Jane's bedroom is like some sort of Picasso painting, a twisted frame. Shadows are painted on walls. The girl herself looks as if she's engulfed in clothes made of spider webs. When Cesare comes to her window, his black clothing and stylized makeup make him look like a Goth kid on his worst day. He enters through a window opening as jagged as dragon's teeth. He first tries to murder Jane—indeed that is what he is supposed to do. It is what he's done all the other times. But even in his stupefied, zombie-like state, her beauty hits him. He can't just stab her. So he grabs her and tries to take her. And it is his undoing. As he abducts her, she screams and alerts the neighbors. Do you think her bed robes look like a *wedding dress?*

Well, beauty kills the beast, as it must. Cesare tries to run, but in his weak condition, he simply cannot. He drops his prize and falls dead (again, in a bizarre and exaggerated fashion). He has died of exhaustion, or perhaps a broken heart.

From a Hollywood perspective, this is probably the climax of the film. Not here. The real villain is Caligari and he still lives. We see a lengthy segment revealing *his* illness. Admittedly, it's a section of the film that you will probably read more about or have discussions about, but let me make some observations and perhaps clarify it a little. While he may be a psychiatrist, Dr. Caligari is more insane than his patients. He's just waiting for something to release the madness. Cesare is it. Get this and don't forget it: *The respected doctor is the real maniac.*

Caligari's personal life is filled with the imagery of perversion and death. The skeleton in his office could simply be a prop placed there to represent his profession, but I don't think so. The piles of ancient books could have been shelved in an impressive professional library, but they *aren't*. His glasses could be a symbol of his impressive intellect, but instead they are constantly used as a prop for the actor to fiddle with, showing his confusion and deception. Everything about the guy is disturbing. He keeps the sleepwalker in a coffin and pops him out almost as if he is some sort of perverted exhibitionist. Especially noteworthy is the scene in which he shows the sleepwalker to Jane—*with glee*, almost as if he is doing something forbidden.

Photofest

On paper, Caligari is an insane killer and Cesare is only his weapon. But visually, there are clear signals indicating that the sleepwalker is some sort of strange love-object. Showing him to someone is akin to an exhibitionist showing his victim something nasty. *The Cabinet of Dr. Caligari* (1920).

The last and most important point to discuss here is the presence of what is called a **Framing Story**. The beginning and end of the picture are told from a different perspective and take place *outside* the narrative in the center of the film.

THE CENTRAL STORY

Two young men wrote a film script chronicling a series of unsolved murders that took place in their hometown. In their story, the murder was a mere pawn being used by a puppet master of sorts. The thing that interested them was the notion that the real culprit was the intellectual, much-admired doctor. Their story had an **antiauthoritarian** streak; it criticized society's leaders and questions all of us for following after them so blindly. The central story we see in *Caligari* (Francis' tale) warns us not to follow blindly after a person simply because he/she seems wise or respected.

Flash forward to the preparation phase of the film and a young man named Fritz Lang was hired to direct.[7] He was eventually replaced because the producers believed he was too inexperienced for the project. But not before he had added one important contribution to the film. Lang suggested what would become known as a "framing story" at the beginning and end of the film. In that frame, the central story was made into a tale told by Francis. The important thing to remember is that Francis is insane—so the central story becomes only the hallucinatory ravings of a madman.

This is perhaps the most important thing to remember about *The Cabinet of Dr. Caligari*. The original story questioned authority and warned society not to follow after leaders blindly. But when the filmmakers positioned this story as merely a tale told by an insane asylum patient, it's as if they are saying, "Oh, but the great doctor Caligari is going to cure everything in the end. We can trust him to take care of us!"

In retrospect, the links to the rise of Hitler and the Nazis are obvious. It's as if *Caligari* is warning us to watch out for the coming leaders and not to trust them. Keep in mind that the film was made roughly 15 years before the Nazi era and that we cannot think they were prophets of some sort. Entire books have been written describing what the film seems to say about fascism, but the authors of these books are doing what we are doing—looking backward on the comparison. The original film authors did indeed have an antiauthoritarian message in their story, but it was much more general. Any government, indeed any organization, is being questioned and challenged by the central story of *Caligari*. What did Fritz Lang and the film's producers intend to say? It is my opinion that they had no intentional desire to remove the film's original antiestablishment message, but only intended to add one more layer of strangeness: tell a weird story and then to top it off, reveal that it's all a hallucination. Just look at the visual design of the framing scenes. They're just as strange as the central story.

Ultimately, *The Cabinet of Dr. Caligari* is fascinating to watch. However, it is even more interesting if you know *what lies behind the screen*.

---

[7] You will be hearing much more about Fritz Lang. He would become one of the greatest filmmakers in the history of cinema.

GIVE ME YOUR FEEDBACK:
THE CABINET OF DR. CALIGARI

1. The original writers' story had a message about the ordinary people admiring and following those with power and authority. What was that original message?

2. The future director, Fritz Lang added a "framing story," which changed the whole meaning of the film. When you consider the framing story, what does the film seem to tell us about ordinary people and how they treat those in authority?

3. Give three examples of set pieces that are expressionistic. How do these sets make us feel?

4. Even the acting of the performers is bizarre and stylized; give three examples of this sort of expressionistic acting.

THE FIRST VAMPIRE FILM: *NOSFERATU*

"Vampires are not pretty
They do not sparkle
They do not date you
They only love you because you taste good"

—Bob Jordan

We can see *Nosferatu* (1922) only by accident.[8] Silent film director, F. W. Murnau is considered today to be one of the great artists of cinema. But back in the day, he did something that seems really, really stupid. Murnau decided to make a vampire film. Specifically, he decided to make a film version of the novel, *Dracula*. The novel was still under copyright, but Murnau decided he could get around that little problem. He changed the character name from Count Dracula to "Orlok." The term vampire is changed to "nosferatu" and the evil creature's minion is changed from Renfield to Knock. Simple plan—and foolproof wasn't it? Well, the Stoker estate sued. *Successfully.* The court ruled that the film was an illegal adaptation of *Dracula* and all prints of the film were ordered destroyed—world-wide. If successful, the picture would never be seen again.

Fortunately, a number of prints of the film had already been distributed internationally when the suit was decided. Had laws worked the way they were supposed to, the film would have been destroyed back in the 1920s. Fortunately, mistakes worked in our favor (for once). And also, the film itself is worth the legend that built up around it. *Nosferatu* is still as creepy, still as full of atmosphere as any vampire film fan might hope.

If you have read the original novel by Bram Stoker, you will quickly realize that Murnau altered, and especially omitted, much of the classic Dracula story. However, the plots are essentially identical and, more important, the spirit of each work is the same. The story chronicles the effort of Dracula, er, Orlok, to move from his remote castle to a major city where he'd have more victims than an evil undead might ever dream of. The vampire's lust for a particular neck—that of a pretty young woman—will lead to his destruction. But more than its storyline, the spirit, the personality of *Nosferatu*, is taken straight from the Stoker novel. The vampire has the dusty, ancient feeling of a hundred-year-old suit found in your grandparents' attic. The castle is just as spooky as any haunted house that Hollywood might present for us.

And if you forget everything else in this essay, remember this: the filmmaker sometimes tries to use special effects and eerie techniques to create a supernatural atmosphere, but they are nothing when compared to his natural cinematography. The Real—the real actor playing Orlok, the real castle, the real rats skittering from a literal ghost ship—those are more disturbing than any special effect.

The story of *Nosferatu* is different to us today than it must have been back in the 1920s. Today telling the tale of a young man traveling to a remote hilltop castle to visit an eccentric named Dracula would signal clearly that the fellow was walking blindly into disaster. But the Stoker novel was not an immediate success following its publication in 1897. It makes more

---

[8] If you are one of those who know that there were Soviet and Hungarian silent Dracula films, in 1920 and 1921 respectively, they are both lost, so please humor me.

sense to look back on the spectator viewing *Nosferatu* in its day, knowing the protagonist's journey was ominous. Knowing he was heading into darkness and evil. But my expectation is that there may have been more mystery in the 1920s. The nature of what awaited him didn't have the predictability we'd experience today. Our hapless protagonist, Hutter, travels to the castle home of Count Orlok and even along the way, his destination strikes fear into the hearts of the locals. Examine the environments created by Murnau. The tavern, the local villagers, the streets. The film has a wonderful spirit of foreboding. This is our first hint at what we are experiencing, not the villagers' stories of a werewolf or a book on vampires. We already know the sort of world created by the filmmaker.

When Hutter attempts to hire a coach to the castle, the drivers stop at the bridge. You almost whisper to yourself, "Abandon hope all ye who enter here." Hutter continues on foot but is picked up by a mysterious driver in an equally foreboding coach. Hutter's ride to the castle might be one of the few sequences in the film that does not age well; it even feels corny to the modern-day viewer. Murnau doesn't need to try so hard. He uses what were then disconcerting special effects to elevate the anxiety. He didn't need to. The remote locale selected by the director. The look of the coach. And the look on Hutter's face is enough to make us uneasy. Glimpsing the predatory face of the anonymous driver is more than enough to know our friend Hutter is dinner!

Hutter's arrival at the castle and Orlok's greeting are one of the best-known sequences in silent cinema. The castle doors open almost like some devouring mouth into hell. The viewer has been waiting to glimpse Count Orlok throughout the whole film and is not disappointed. This actor, a mysterious fellow named Max Schreck, is as eerie as anyone you will see in the history of film. When you read about the movement called German expressionism, this moment captures it wonderfully. F. W. Murnau is known as one of cinema's greatest artists. *This is Murnau.*

The casting of a particular actor in a role can be critical. It's almost impossible to imagine someone else playing Vito Corleone in *The Godfather* or Bogart in *Casablanca*. Max Schreck was in other films, but it is likely that this is the only time you will ever see him. But it is enough. You may never forget Schreck and despite the popularity of Bela Lugosi, it is entirely possible that you will think of Count Orlok when someone mentions the name Dracula.

Hutter's visit at the castle is worth close attention. Today, many viewers are likely simply to chuckle at the clichés: the vampire's obsession with a photo of a woman with a lovely neck, the fascination he shows with his visitor's blood. But other images create and enhance the mood, as well: Hutter stumbles back to collapse on a chair with Orlok looming over him, as if to assault him. Hutter's bedroom makes us feel almost as if he is a prison cell. Rats in coffins.

Nosferatu is first and foremost a prime example of the German expressionist movement. As such, the scenes most worthy of our attention are in the castle and later on board the doomed ship. Expressionist films are noteworthy in two ways: the dark themes and the shadowy cinematography. As one considers expressionist stories, doom and pessimism are common. These are stories of monsters, nightmares and the occult. In the case of *Nosferatu*, almost from the first scenes of the film, we can tell that our protagonist is walking into the shadow of death. Visually, the film continues to impress. A highly respected film critic has called the film a sort of visual poetry.[9] Watching the first mate, one of the last surviving men on the ghost ship, as he descends into the hold of the ship still gives chills.

It is often difficult for the modern viewer to relate to a film as old as this. *Nosferatu* is best when considered in the context of its time. We are not trying to compare it with a modern film (and to find it lacking). This is a film with a language of its own. And if you think of it in that context, it ages just as well as a haunting piece of music or an eerie novel.

Notable mention:
Shadow of the Vampire (2000)
Makes a wonderful double feature with *Nosferatu*.
I don't want to spoil anything,
but these films are great fun shown together!

---

[9] Lotte Eisner, *Murnau* (London: Secker and Warburg, 1973), 27.

Name: _____ Date: _____

GIVE ME YOUR FEEDBACK:
NOSFERATU

1. I know you do not find this film scary, but what scene do you still find creepy?

2. How does the director, Murnau, use light and dark to create evil or safe places in the story?

3. Look up F. W. Murnau online. If you wanted to see more films by this director, which ones do you find mentioned that you might be most interested to see?

METROPOLIS (1927)

First and foremost, Fritz Lang's 1927 film *Metropolis* is a science-fiction film. In fact, it is easily one of the most important science-fiction films ever made. It is probably the first motion picture one would consider for its portrayal of a future world (and terms like "dystopian" and "new bad future" would quickly enter the conversation). However, I would argue that it is equally at home, here in our discussion of expressionism. Remembering that German expressionism relied upon two major elements—a dark, eerie visual design and a pessimistic, doomed worldview—*Metropolis* is an expressionist masterwork. As you watch the film, or read this essay, note items that stand out to you as examples of expressionism in *Metropolis*.

Metropolis begins with a very obvious comparison. The world of the film is divided into two social segments: the haves and have-nots, if you will. There is a working class living in underground caverns who are little more than slaves. Taking advantage of their blood, sweat, and tears is an elite class, living lives of privilege and leisure. Director **Fritz Lang** uses a variety of elements at his disposal to communicate the differences between these two classes. The fact that the workers live underground and the elite live under a beautiful sky is obvious. But specific locations and activities quickly catch our attention as well. The workers are surrounded by rock and machinery. Their work makes them seem like machines themselves—cogs in the huge engines. The elite participate in athletic contests and enjoy luxurious parks.

The workers are all the same—drones without individuality. The young men of privilege are not only individuals and achieve unique achievements, but are awarded "companions" for what I loosely call "social entertainment." (*The kind that apparently requires transparent clothing.*)

ANALYSIS

Perhaps the first thing a film fan will learn is that *Metropolis* has gone through many lengths and versions. After a poor initial reception, the film was cut and for many years, roughly a quarter was believed lost. Several major restorations have been attempted, including even one by Giorgio Moroder (music scores for *Midnight Express*, *American Gigolo*), featuring pop performers such as Pat Benetar and Freddie Mercury.[10] Several other, more traditional restorations have returned the film to an almost complete condition. Whichever version of the film one sees, some of the same scenes will stand out. Fritz Lang was one of the most visual of filmmakers and *Metropolis* is full of iconic images, some of them recognized even by folks who have never seen the film.

The workers march to and from work and Lang uses every visual element to tell us they are slaves: their uniforms, their identical bald heads, even their body language. The chosen sons are a direct visual contrast. They are in a beautiful surface world, which the workers will never see.

---

[10] Called the Moroder version, this production was extremely controversial. The music distracted from the visual experience and the running speed of the film was considered to be too fast. However, despite the problems, the Moroder version brought the film back into the public consciousness and probably spurred the more authentic restorations to come.

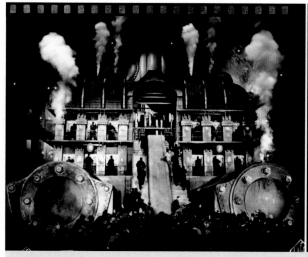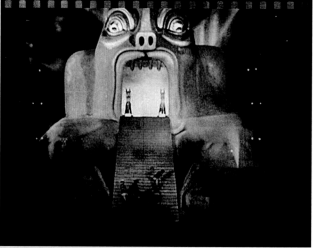

UFA/Photofest

A strange transformation. The machinery is horrifying even in its original state—massive and soul-crushing. But a hallucination (dare I say it, a spiritual vision) makes us see it as a devouring monster, a demon devouring the workers like so much food. *Metropolis* (1927).

As we begin to assimilate the life of the privileged sons, we are introduced to Maria (Brigitte Helm). She is immediately presented as several things: she is mysterious and alluring, a spiritual messiah and a social leader. Most important, the viewer notes the words she says. To the children, "Look, these are your brothers and sisters" and to the elite "these are *your* brothers and sisters."

The elite have space and perform in activities that allow for free action and we even see the sky from time to time. The workers are packed together and live in what are essentially boxes. Cold stone is shown everywhere.

But it is the workers' machines that interest viewers the most. They are huge and dwarf the humans. Even in their original forms, they are frightening, monstrous. Many words have been devoted to descriptions of director Fritz Lang, but "subtle" is not one of them. It is extremely easy to understand that the workers are merely part of the machinery. They are pieces—and sad, disposable ones at that.

When our hero, Freder, finds his way into the world of the workers, he has a vision of the true nature of the workers' machines. Remember when it was argued earlier that this science fiction film is an important part of the expressionist movement? Freder's nightmarish vision is a powerful example of this. The machine turns into a demon, Moloch, an ancient deity. And it devours the workers like so much food. Even today, it is a striking image. To me it seems like *this* is the moment when this science fiction story turns into something strange and distorted. Freder's journey will become more and more unnatural—indeed, supernatural. And as we witness his madness, indeed as we enter his mind, we even see gods come to life.

A critic could likely write a brief essay on virtually any scene in the entire film (and even some essays that would be not-so-brief). But for now, jump forward a bit and notice the introduction of the character Rotwang. Notice his house. Notice his costume and hair. Lang even portrays him having lost a hand, dressed in black.[11] He is a mad scientist. The look, especially the acting style of Friedrich Rudolf Klein-Rogge reminds one of Caligari's monster, Caesar. Exaggerated. Stylized. Distorted. Soon, Rotwang will be playing with Maria, almost like a cat playing with his mouse—in a tomb full of skulls.[12]

Themes and messages are difficult to discern in some films. In *Metropolis*, they are everywhere and

---

[11] Remember, we may laugh today when we think of other mad scientist characters with the same affectation. Dr. Strangelove comes quickly to mind, but they came later. Don't include your thoughts of the parodies and the copies as you consider a subject that came earlier.

[12] Ironically, Klein-Rogge was married to Thea von Harbou, who would leave him for director Fritz Lang. So Lang and Klein-Rogge had a conflict over a woman, just as Joh Fredersen and Rotwang have in the film.

are impossible to miss. The most impact comes with continuous religious symbolism. When Freder explores the workers' caves, he takes a man's shift and it quickly becomes clear that he is not just suffering, he is being crucified. The real Maria leads a religious meeting and Freder responds, taking upon himself a mission of reunification.

The most noteworthy scene is once again one of Freder's visions. In this one, he is at the sanctuary and statues of Death and the Seven Deadly Sins come to life.

As an actor, Brigitte Helm had the chance to give, not just one memorable performance, but two. Religious symbolism and the disturbing themes of expressionism come to a head with the character of Maria. The real Maria is an angel. The false Maria is a siren, a beautiful monster. Helm had the rare opportunity to play both virgin and whore in one film. For readers who are not familiar with the reference, the false Maria riding on the backs of the dragon statues at the Yoshiwara club is a Biblical image, the beautiful seductress who leads us to our doom.

A FALSE CONCLUSION

The final thought I wish to leave with you is this: the resolution of the film—the way all the problems are tied-up—is false. Of the many criticisms of the film, this seems to have the most important ramifications. The entire social structure of the city of Metropolis is unjust. A small elite lives in luxury and the rest are basically slaves. In the end of the film, Maria improves the workers' lives marginally, but there is no question that Metropolis will continue. Its elite will still enjoy the eternal gardens and the workers will be needed to run the machines. Granted, perhaps Maria has improved their working conditions, but I see no hint that their lot in life will be changed significantly. After all, Maria's "sermon" on the original Tower of Babel completely misses the point, doesn't it?

Metropolis was one of Adolf Hitler's favorite films. Clearly, he missed the point as well. He liked the whole notion that some special people had the right to live in luxury while the rest of the world served them. He liked the huge, dramatic scope of the film—*Metropolis* as spectacle. Indeed, this sort of size and drama would come to life in his own vision of Nazi cinema: we need only to see *Triumph of the Will*. To me, both films are only partly about content—they are remembered primarily as breathtaking filmic language.

Post-script: Legendary author H. G. Welles hated *Metropolis* and called it one of the silliest films he'd ever seen.

GIVE ME YOUR FEEDBACK:
METROPOLIS

1. Why does your author believe the character Maria has completely misinterpreted the story of the Tower of Babel?

2. What examples of eerie, supernatural images did you notice that support the notion that this is an expressionist film?

   — The machine turning into an ancient Diety and eating people

3. Why would Hitler like this film so much?

SILENT GERMANY— A STEP FURTHER

In some cases, an important film movement will stand alone, surrounded by material that is much less significant. In a few cases, material following after that major film movement needs to be addressed as well, at least in passing. Expressionism was arguably the most significant type of cinema in the history of Germany. However, it gave rise to additional, smaller movements that were also important. German silent cinema after expressionism is remarkable as well. However, as one studies the films that followed after expressionism, they seem to call for a different approach. The films that are remembered from what might be called Post-Expressionist Cinema, are the works of particular individuals. The notion that the study of history is merely the study of a series of Great Men is often criticized, but it is the easiest way to address this material. We will go a step further than simply limiting our study to expressionism, but do so only in the most basic and limited manner. Following German expressionism, we will note the work of several filmmakers. I know we will miss a great deal, but we will touch on several masters who need to be included.

F. W. MURNAU

He was imperious, demanding, aloof.[13] He was openly gay in a time when many filmmakers would not publicize such things. F. W. Murnau is often thought of as the most artistic filmmaker of the silent era. His film career began even before the time of expressionism and he continued to surprise and awe until his untimely accidental death.

As was mentioned earlier, one of Murnau's most famous films is the vampire classic, *Nosferatu*. With it and a number of lesser films, he stands as a giant in the expressionistic movement.[14] But his career would grow far beyond that movement.

Perhaps it was the bizarre, unnatural subject matter in German expressionism, but it gave rise to a smaller style of film called **kammerspielfilm**, loosely translated as "intimate theater." These films chronicle the story of everyday life of the poor and forgotten. The movement itself is forgotten as well, save for one film, *The Last Laugh* (a.k.a. *The Last Man*, 1924).[15] *The Last Laugh* is considered by many to be the greatest silent film ever made and is even regarded as one of the very greatest pictures in the entire history of cinema.

In direct contrast to the monsters and madmen of the expressionist movement, *The Last Laugh* offers us a small, everyday kind of story. It chronicles the experiences of a lower-class working man whose only claim to fame in his little world is that he is the doorman at a grand luxury hotel. His pride isn't just "worn on his sleeve," as the expression might run; it literally *is* his sleeve—he wears a grand uniform, which makes him special in his neighborhood. It doesn't seem like much of a film premise—certainly not that of a masterwork. But it is the way Murnau tells his story, not the story itself, that elevates it above most cinema. The first thing the viewer notices is that the film has no inter-title cards. The

---

[13] And he stood 6'11", probably adding to this intimidation-factor greatly!

[14] Of special note here is the 1927 film *Faust* that features some of the most impressive images seen in a silent film.

[15] The German title, *Der letzte Mann* and the proper translation, *The Last Man*, are less well-known than *The Last Laugh*, so this English title will be used throughout the essay.

No monsters. No spiritual visions. No insanity. *The Last Laugh* is a wordless examination of the lives of The Little People. It is the story of doorman at a luxury hotel. His life and pride (and the respect he enjoys from his neighbors) all revolve around that job—and the greatcoat that comes with it. A silly coat. But if it were ever taken from him, his whole life would be without meaning. *The Last Laugh* (1924).

story, including an understanding of how the protagonist feels, is all told visually. People in this era referred to silent cinema as a "universal language" and *The Last Laugh* is one of the greatest examples of that achievement.

Once one realizes the film does not use words to communicate, the viewer considers the cinematography in a different manner. We realize that we are seeing images that are carefully composed to include all the information Murnau intends to give us—in a single shot. It is the same material some directors (then or now) might need to chop into small pieces in order to tell the story.

The film is renowned for its moving camera. One of the most rewarding parts of viewing *The Last Laugh* is for the viewer to watch the way the camera moves— through streets, up elevators, through buildings. It is magical. Truly, that one element transforms this from the ordinary to the beautiful. It also helps us to understand the character and feel drawn into the film. A first-person camera would essentially become the character, emulating his visual point of view. Murnau doesn't do that, but what he does is make the camera a character itself. It's as if we the viewers are given the chance to "shadow" the fellow and watch

his work duties, see his hotel, follow him home. We travel along with him—and sometimes that means pausing to look at him, but it especially means moving along with him. A great French director, Marcel Carné, remembers being influenced by Murnau. "The camera … glides, rises, zooms or weaves where the story takes it. It is no longer fixed, but takes part in the action and becomes a character in the drama."[16]

Anytime a film focuses almost exclusively on one player, that performer needs to give a truly compelling performance. Legendary actor Emil Jannings plays the Doorman (who is given no name) with great pomp and self-importance. Jannings' performances have often been criticized as bombastic and over-large, but it seems a perfect fit here. His performance expresses how his character feels about himself. Personally, I think it's one of his best performances. And the way he puffs up whenever his neighbors see him, actually helps me empathize with the character. If Jannings had kept his pride in control, just letting it slip out occasionally, I would have a different opinion toward the Doorman. This isn't a particularly bright man and certainly not a man who examines himself—I think he is lovable in part because his personality flaw is so obvious and he is, well, so oblivious.

So as the viewer sees the film, it becomes quickly evident that the story is simple and less than captivating. What makes it a great film? What makes it so important? The performance. The composition of the image. And especially the camera movement. It will be an influential model for many of the films to come and it will always represent the potential of silent cinema.

The Last Laugh was successful and highly regarded as an artistic masterwork. Murnau was able to fund larger films afterward. But the director's artistic prowess drew notice, not just in Europe, but America as well. Hollywood called to the imperious artist and he would make his last masterpiece for an American studio.

Looking to increase his studio's artistic standing, the mogul William Fox brought Murnau to Hollywood. His first film for Fox continues to be judged as one of the greatest films in history, even today. *Sunrise* (1927) was the simple story of a love triangle. A country man with a loyal wife is seduced by a sexual siren and the dreams of a better life. In the end, he sees the

---

[16] John Wakeman. *World Film Directors, Volume 1* (The H. W. Wilson Company, 1987), 812.

error of his ways and comes to cherish his wife and receive her forgiveness. Like the Doorman, these are little people and their stories are of no great importance in the world, but Murnau tells their tale in a way that makes them very real—even precious—to us. And their story comes to represent something about life for everyman.

Again, the viewer will grow to appreciate the film due, not to the story, but due to Murnau's masterful style. Examine the cinematography, especially shots of the city, which was actually a forced-perspective set, scaled specifically for the way Murnau envisioned the place. Intertitles are at a minimum and tracking shots are frequent. Frankly, *Sunrise* is simply a visual poem.

The film may not have achieved commercial success, but even in the 1920s, *Sunrise* was seen as one of the greatest works of art ever placed on a movie screen. The film was given a special Best Artistic Production Academy Award (at the time, considered to be equal in importance to the Outstanding Picture Award given to the film *Wings*).

It must have seemed that Murnau was entering yet another successful chapter in his remarkable film career, but it would be another of those "What Might Have Been" stories so common throughout history. Three films followed *Sunrise*, but one is damaged, one lost and the third is largely considered to be marred by artistic conflict. In the end, *Sunrise* would stand as the last of Murnau's great films and virtually our last taste of his abilities. In 1931, he was killed in an auto accident. He was 42 years old.

FRITZ LANG

Fritz Lang has been named "The Master of Darkness" by the British Film Institute. His best films would make a wonderful winter film series (somehow they just seem to be winter films, not summer): *Metropolis, The Weary Death, M, Fury, Scarlet Street, The Big Heat, and Rancho Notorious*. Through his works, we see the transition from German expressionism to American film noir.

We have already examined the first of Lang's masterworks, *Metropolis*, and seen its importance to the science fiction genre as well as the German expressionist movement. As I mentioned, it was one of Adolf Hitler's favorite films (for all the wrong reasons). According to one version of the story, he had propaganda minister Joseph Goebbels approach Fritz Lang, inviting him to become head of the Nazi film program. Being half-Jewish, Lang wisely turned down the job offer and left Germany soon thereafter.

His wife stayed. And became an ardent Nazi.

Prior to his arrival in the United States, Fritz Lang made one other world-renowned film, simply entitled *M*. Once in America, he became a highly-respected and prolific Hollywood director. He claimed afterwards to dislike *Metropolis*. Was it because of the Nazis' fascination with the film? Was it because he found the story to be naïve? No one will ever know.

G. W. PABST AND STREET REALISM

Along with the "small stories" told by *kammerspielfilm*, the lives of poor and forgotten were the focus for G. W. Pabst. His films were called **street realism** and can be thought of today as a type of cynical social criticism.

Pabst tells stories of the dirty underside of Germany—and it's easy to see how they may cause some viewers to see them as the soil that gave root to Nazism. Pay particular attention to the mise-en scene (the environment, the world) of his films. They are dark. The world they show is full of the forgotten and the damned. Some of his best-known films focus on the lives of women in these dirty streets: *Pandora's Box* and *Diary of a Lost Girl* (both 1927), *The Joyless*

It doesn't really matter if characters in "street realism" are living the high-life or are down and out on the dark streets, they are in the gutter. *Pandora's Box* (1929) features legendary film star Louise Brooks who brought a sexy-but-sad cynicism to her performances.

Street (1925). While overshadowed by the surreal worlds of the expressionist films and the fascinating cinematography of *The Last Laugh*, Pabst is one of the greatest directors of the 20th Century and his worlds of street realism deserve to be well-remembered.

THE NAZI CURTAIN FALLS

I do not have the time or the desire to give a detailed analysis of the next stage in German cinema. The Nazis come and film becomes a propaganda tool. At its worst, some Nazi films are simply revolting lies attempting to prove that Jews are subhuman. At the best, well, even today, *Triumph of the Will* (1935) is awe-inspiring and terrifying in its visual power. Both sides in the war used that same film as propaganda: the Nazis used it to show how powerful they were—and thus inspire their followers. The Allies used it to show how powerful the Nazis were also—but to help soldiers understand what we were fighting to stop.

Horrifying. Inspiring. Dramatic. This film was used by the Nazis to increase morale and also used by Allied Forces to show the fanatical enemy they were fighting. Do you see how even something like the *Star Wars* films were inspired by this kind of imagery? *Triumph of the Will* (1935).

Contemporary Films Ltd./Photofest

GIVE ME YOUR FEEDBACK:
POST-EXPRESSIONIST GERMANY

1. In *The Last Laugh*, the ending of the film is often criticized as being out-of-place, or even phony. What is the event that is added in the epilogue and do you feel it is a good ending or a poor one—and why?

2. How did German director F. W. Murnau fare when he came to Hollywood? Are any of his films considered significant today?

3. Why would the Allies of WWII show the Nazi film *Triumph of the Will* to their own soldiers?

MONTAGE FILMS OF THE SOVIET UNION

"For us, film is the most important art."

—Vladimir Lenin

For the purposes of silent film study, the Soviet Revolution of 1917 can be broken into two parts. In the first phase, during February and March of 1917, the Russian Tsar was overthrown. Groups with radically (excuse the pun) different beliefs joined together in their common hatred of the Tsar's government. Once the Tsar had been ousted, a provisional government, led by Alexander Kerensky, was established. But made up of an assortment of groups that hated each other, it was doomed to failure from the start. In October of 1917, the Kerensky government was replaced by the Bolsheviks. The cynic in me notes that the Bolsheviks may not have been the largest party, but their passion was unstoppable.

Vladimir Lenin was cinema's greatest political champion, perhaps ever. He stated, "For us, film is the most important art." This is an important notion to consider. The new Soviet Union was huge. It was composed of dozens of separate peoples—most of whom spoke different languages. Most of them were illiterate. How would you communicate with such a vast assortment of people? A book? A series of speeches? Movies were the perfect solution for the Bolsheviks to transmit their beliefs. Lenin understood that cinema would be a key part of the revolution.

But the whole medium had been embraced (the Soviets would probably say "co-opted") by capitalists. Films were a commercial product, intended to attract a wide audience and make massive amounts of money for their producers. It was the very antithesis of what Lenin envisioned. A new type of cinema was needed—one that served the revolution, not capitalist profitmaking.

In retrospect we can see the answer: film would need to reject the narrative entertainment form and replace it with a political debate—an argument of sorts. The solution would be found through editing. At a Moscow film school (the first of its kind), a professor would play an important role in the development of this revolutionary cinema. **Lev Kuleshov** was unconventional, even in the radical world of the Soviet Union in the post-World War I era. He believed the power of cinema was in editing. He is remembered today, not for his films, but for his editing experiments—his lecture illustrations, if you will. In the best-known of these "Kuleshov Experiments," he linked together the passive face of an actor with an emotional image, such as children playing in a park or a graveside funeral. His point was that the result was not just the two images set together—it became something different—something more powerful. Viewers of these experiments believed the actor was heartbroken or happy, based on the juxtaposition of the two images. The editing had created a new meaning for the images.

Sitting in the classroom were some of the Soviet Union's new generation of filmmakers, most notably Pudovkin and Eisenstein. As is so often the case, the professor may be a distant memory while his students achieved fame, but Kuleshov was a critical inspiration for these great masters. With his lessons on the true power of cinematic language, Pudovkin and Eisenstein would move forward and use them to express their own perspectives on the revolution.

PUDOVKIN

Of three filmmakers we will address from the Soviet Montage era, Vsevolod Pudovkin is the least well-known today. Pudovkin is often contrasted with Eisenstein because they came from the same movement, shared some of the same education, and promoted the same political cause, but they do so in very different ways. Eisenstein's films are very cerebral, almost mathematical. In contrast, Pudovkin focused on the power of the individual, even recognizing heroism. To be honest, I am surprised that today he is not better recognized in the West. His films seem to me much more accessible to our sensibilities.

In the late silent era, Pudovkin directed three films, a political trilogy of sorts, which are each considered to be among the greatest films of Soviet history. *Mother* (1926) is the adaptation of a Maxim Gorky novel and shows the revolution against the Tsar through the story of a single family. It was followed by two equally-respected films, *The End of Saint Petersburg* (1927) and *Storm Over Asia* (1928). A scene from *The End of Saint Petersburg* is worth note here. The capitalist greed of the St. Petersburg stock exchange is juxtaposed with common-man soldiers dying in World War I. It is a very standard telling of the Bolshevik version of history: the proletariat bleeds while the capitalists profit from their pain. Editing powerfully links the poor soldiers' deaths with the forward rush of capitalists looking only for profit. But it is typical. If that is all Pudovkin could accomplish, he would not be remembered and studied today. In fact, he accomplishes much more. His stories have a human side—he offers not just the "party line" propaganda, but tells a much more engaging, human story as well. Note this dimension when examining *Mother*.

Poor health and criticism from the Stalin regime worked together to make Pudovkin's career lessen in both quantity and quality in the sound era.

EISENSTEIN

Sergei Eisenstein is one of the most important figures in the history of cinema—both as a filmmaker and as a film theorist. His writings are still translated and studied today and his films are still considered to be among the greatest of intellectual works. Perhaps no

My favorite photo of Sergei Eisenstein. Something about the fact that a communist revolutionary would be sitting on a royal throne of the regime he helped overthrow—and that he is "kicking back" as if it's his easy chair. When I think of Eisenstein I think of his brilliance, but also his precociousness and unshakable belief in himself.

one else has been as highly regarded as a writer *and* as a director as well. His writings are extremely eclectic. An essay might include references to figures such as Charlie Chaplin and Charles Dickens, or compare Japanese art with cinema. While his films are full of powerful, even experimental, editing techniques, one can also study them as photography. I often watch an Eisenstein film in the classroom and have students comment that his still composition is quite beautiful.

Eisenstein is by far the most important filmmaker in the history of the Soviet Union. Rather than a masterwork or two during his career, a film student could very well examine a dozen different films. Among them, *The Battleship Potemkin* is perhaps the most famous (and will be addressed here in depth), but *October: Ten Days That Shook the World* and *Strike* might be almost as frequently studied. Later in his career, Eisenstein directed two parts of a planned trilogy on Ivan the Terrible and his epic *Alexander Nevsky* is considered to be a national treasure. As with Pudovkin, Eisenstein's work was frustrated by political attacks and poor health. He died of a heart attack at just age fifty.[17]

---

[17] Eisenstein's primary political foe was Executive Producer of Soviet Cinema, Boris Shumatsky. Throughout the 1930s, Shumatsky waged an extremely personal battle against Eisenstein, but in the end, the filmmaker's career was salvaged and Shumatsky was executed as a traitor.

DZIGA VERTOV

Dziga Vertov (whose real name was David Kaufman a.k.a. Denis, but is known by his Vertov pseudonym) was not a student of Kuleshov's. He was the editor of news reels following the Revolution. Even in the world of early Soviet cinema, he was always the radical. His writings are ferociously anti-narrative. He called story films a "corrupting influence" on the proletarian sensibility. He called it a drug for the masses. As he edited films, and later as he made his own, he believed that cinema could help man evolve into a higher form of being—a form with less human imperfection and more machine precision. He believed the camera was an eye, but an eye without the limitations of the human one. And he believed that it would show us the Truth. The title of one of Vertov's best-known film series, *Kino Pravda* literally means Film Truth.

While in recent years a number of Vertov's works have begun to be appreciated, he will always be remembered for *Man with the Movie Camera* (1929), a film that is often linked with the handful of "City Symphony" films made in the silent era. *Man with the Movie Camera* truly illustrates Vertov's goal of making a new language for cinema. Like many films of this sort, *Man with the Movie Camera* shows us a city from dawn until dark—its people, its machines, its buildings. Where this film is different, and indeed special, is in *what* it chooses to show and *how* it shows that material. The film opens and closes with an audience arriving at a movie theater to see a film. We see the silent film orchestra warming up and the spectators taking their seats. We even see the projectionist beginning to run the film. It is as if we are watching the very film they are seeing! Anyone familiar with a film like *Berlin: Symphony of a Great City* is familiar with some images: cleaning ladies readying stores for the new day, traffic taking to the streets, but here Vertov continually reminds us we are watching a film. We see a cameraman going out into the street to find subjects to photograph. We even see the footage he has apparently shot on his outing. Later we will see an editor hard at work splicing the celluloid. We see the actual images as they are being cut. *Man with the Movie Camera* is an early example of a technique that has been extremely popular since the 1960s: **self-reflexivity**. A self-reflexive film reminds us that we are watching cinema and indeed draws attention to the fact that a film is a manipulated art form, not reality—not Truth. Self-reflexivity can be small things: a character who calls himself Roy Rogers or one who talks directly to the film audience.[18] Dziga Vertov amps it up significantly. In one well-known sequence, a woman wakes up and blinks her eyes. Vertov links that with window blinds, that are opening and closing, and also with a camera iris as it opens and closes. You honestly cannot watch *Man with the Movie Camera* without continually thinking about the fact that you are watching a film. It is believed that viewers are more critical, more intellectually active, when they are not just passively watching a story.

Man with the Movie Camera is a film full of contradictions. Vertov called it "life as it is" and "life caught unawares" but parts are clearly staged. Many of the people shown in the film are clearly aware of the presence of the camera. The film is full of manipulation by the filmmakers—including fast- and slow-motion shots and actions that had to have been repeated multiple times for the camera.

Dziga Vertov experienced more success in the sound film era than some of the other well-known silent directors. *Enthusiasm: Symphony of the Donbass* (1931) and *Three Songs about Lenin* (1934) are both highly regarded works, even today. However, the coming of Stalin's "Soviet Realism" spelled the end for Vertov's creative control. He died of cancer in 1954, but he ended his career, much as he began it, as a propaganda film editor.

END OF AN ERA

The filmmakers of the Soviet silent era believed the absence of narrative would make viewers more active intellectually, but the result is often propaganda—films that try to give *one* specific message and drive it home with all the subtlety of a sledgehammer. With the coming of Stalin, even that form of expression was eliminated. This is just my opinion, but it seems to me that Stalin did not personally understand the montage films of the silent era and he felt threatened by what he didn't understand.[19] What he ushered in to replace it was a style called **Soviet Realism**, but the films are unimportant and, indeed, the Soviet cinema would be unimportant for the next 30 years.

---

[18] Yes, those are actual examples, *Die Hard* and *Ferris Bueller's Day Off* (among many others).

[19] Take for example, Stalin's reactions to Eisenstein's major films *Ivan the Terrible*, Parts 1 & 2. He was impressed by the first film, but when he learned the tyrannical character Ivan was intended to represent him, the second film met with his anger.

THE BATTLESHIP POTEMKIN (1925)

Ask any film scholar on the planet and they will assuredly tell you that *The Battleship Potemkin* (1925) by **Sergei Eisenstein** is one of the most important films ever made. True, it is a great example of propaganda. Yes, it includes some excellent examples of the sort of montage editing for which the Soviets were famous. But what seems most interesting to me is why Eisenstein even made this film in the first place!

The Battleship Potemkin tells the story of the mutiny on board a Russian naval ship in 1905. Think about just that fact. A story about a ship—from 1905. The topic that should matter most to a Soviet film director is the Revolution, which took place in 1917, right?

Why would the greatest of those Soviet directors choose this story?

It is an allegory—a look at the Revolution in miniature. The mutinous sailors on the Potemkin represent the proletariat, the common folks and how they are persecuted and rebel. It is a preview of the grand nationwide rebellion that would take place 15 years later. Once one understands this, the film makes perfect sense.

THE PLOT

As is so often the case in life, this story starts with rancid meat. Yes, I'm actually being serious, at least in relation to this film. The officers on the Tsar's battleship, Potemkin, brutalize the sailors and basically treat them like slaves, but the last straw really comes when the sailors are given only spoiled provisions. And when they refuse to eat the rancid,

maggot-infested meat, the captain orders them executed! The firing squad is assembled, but they refuse to fire on their comrades and the mutiny is on.

With the law of large numbers on their side, the sailors quickly overpower the officers and take the ship. However, a charismatic leader of the sailors, Vakulinchuk, is killed.

While it is by no means the climax of the film, the next stage is one of the most significant sections of the story. The battleship cannot stay at sea forever—it must dock. The Potemkin pulls into the port of Odessa. Remember, these are mutineers who have committed treason by taking the battleship. What do they expect when they come into port? Arrest and execution! What they get instead is a warm welcome. Understand that for Eisenstein, this is one of the most significant elements of the story. The way the sailors were treated by the officers is exactly the same way that the commoners of Odessa are treated by the Tsar and his soldiers. The common folk, the proletariat, empathize with those abused sailors and welcome them with open arms. The Revolution is growing. It is only 1905 and we know in retrospect that it won't succeed then, but for Eisenstein this tiny little incident represents so much more. The fire is catching and eventually it will spread!

Once they have received a warm welcome from the people of Odessa (and not arrest!) the sailors bring the body of Vakulinchuk to shore where he is laid in state in a crude tent by the shore. To me this is actually the weakest portion of the film, but the reason why I see it this way is significant. Vakulinchuk was a critical character in the early parts of the film. In

Hollywood, a leading star like James Cagney would be cast in the role.[20] Given that the character dies in the middle of the story, Hollywood might even bring back his image at key points to remind us that his spirit and his sacrifice drive this rebellion! But for the filmmakers of the Soviet Union, Eisenstein included, notions like valorizing the individual as a hero (much less casting a Hollywood star to play him) is a huge problem. The Soviet Revolution is supposed be about the proletariat. All of the people working together. The group, not the individual. So Eisenstein makes little effort to build up Vakulinchuk as a well-defined protagonist. Yes, he is given important and inspiring lines of propaganda, but he is really just one of the sailors. Eisenstein achieves his goal (avoiding the glamorizing of individual heroism), but there is a price in the middle of the film. We care less for Vakulinchuk and his sacrifice and frankly, this could be the body of any Potemkin sailor—or 20—in terms of creating audience empathy. But honestly, that is the reason viewers today (especially those in the West) might look at this scene and mutter, "So what?"

It comes as no surprise to the film viewer—the Tsar cannot just sit by and watch an entire city break into open rebellion. But it still shocks today, decades later. The enthusiastic people of Odessa gather on the grand theater steps where they can see the ship and wave encouragement to their brave comrades. The Tsar's solders march in and quell the rebellion—with great of ferocity. "The Odessa Steps" section is the best-known part of the film and indeed one of the best-known sequences in all of cinema. Pay close attention to the editing. The brutality of the attack is all about editing that I will just call "visceral." In many cases, we don't actually see the most graphic violence—we feel it through the editing. A woman shot in the face. A baby in a carriage slashed to death by a Cossack's saber. If they were done with 1925 special effects or corny camera tricks, we'd be laughing today. Instead, we are hit by Eisenstein's editing almost as if we were being slapped in the face. No one in the theater is laughing.

It must be in *The Evil Overlord Handbook*. The Tsar's plan doesn't just go after the people of Odessa, but also attempts to take out the battleship Potemkin itself. A squadron of loyalist Russian ships attacks the rebellious battleship and attempts to cut off its escape. Again, we see the subtext of the story, which clearly fascinated Eisenstein. After a tense few minutes, the Russian squad lets the Potemkin escape, calling the mutineers, "Brothers!" Again, a Soviet propagandist sees this as a spark of rebellion that will lead to the eventual events of 1917. For now, the battleship Potemkin sails off into history and the film audience is left knowing full-well that it will take time, but the Revolution they fought for will eventually succeed.

THE EDITING

Any discussion of Eisenstein (indeed of any well-known silent Soviet filmmaker) will begin and end with one element of the equation: editing. Eisenstein's writings on film are just as important today as his films. In those writings, he described several different types of montage. Trying to keep it simple, montage links different images together through the use of editing. These comparisons may be as simple as a child on a swing flowing back and forth, followed immediately by a shot of a clock pendulum swinging with exactly the same rhythm. It might also have complex meaning. If I link an image of children chasing each other with sticks and follow it with a photo of warriors charging with spears, it creates a new meaning—that children's aggressive play leads to violence and even war when they grow up.

The latter form of montage, the one that creates a new, charged meaning through the collision of those images, Eisenstein calls "**intellectual montage**." Personally, I believe his film *October* (1927) includes the best examples of the technique, but we see some very interesting ones in *Battleship Potemkin* as well. During the mutiny on board the ship, note the way a priest waves his crucifix threateningly and how it is then compared with an officer brandishing his saber in a similar manner. It not only gives the priest's actions a menacing tone, but also clearly signals his alliance with the officers (and the Orthodox Church's support of the Tsar as well). All in a simple pair of images shown together.

The very best-known example of montage in *Potemkin* is a very simple one, but it goes by so quickly that I will mention it here. As the big guns on the

---

20 Some of you may not know the popular stars of the studio era, so allow me to update the example. In the modern era, I might cast someone like Chris Evans of Captain America fame. He is sincere and passionate, he is a natural leader—you get the idea.

battleship open up on the soldiers, there is a quick sequence of three statues of lions. The first is sleeping. The second is awake and looking around. The third stands and roars. It is as if the lion is coming to life. It very well might be Eisenstein's way of saying, "Even the very stones cry out in anger when they see this brutal massacre!"

THE PROPAGANDA

Obviously, *The Battleship Potemkin* is a classic propaganda piece. Ironically, Eisenstein and other Soviet directors hated films that they believed made viewers passive and uninvolved. Their works are an attempt to "activate" the audience and get them engaged in the subject matter of the film (in this case, obviously, the Revolution). But in their attempt to make viewers active intellectually, they actually create one of the most blatant, strident of film styles that I have ever seen. Far from allowing a viewer to engage his/her brain and make judgements and interpretations for themselves, films like *Battleship Potemkin* practically shove their message down our throats. I don't consider that to be the experience of an intellectually active film viewer. But as a propaganda piece, it does its job, making the sides clear and the cause worthy.

So I conclude where I began some pages ago. Vladimir Lenin stated, "For us, film is the most important art!" He was leading a Revolution in a land that covers thousands of miles, dozens of different languages and cultures, a largely illiterate population—in a time when there was basically no other form of electronic media to draw upon. And the films of Sergei Eisenstein were the perfect tool.

GIVE ME YOUR FEEDBACK:
THE BATTLESHIP POTEMKIN

1. Why is it important to include a priest who supports the captain and officers on board the Potemkin? Does he represent anything about Russia in general?

2. Are there any specific incidents on board the ship that cause you to relate to the sailors and make you angry at their conditions and the way the officers treat them?

3. What individual people are recognized on the Odessa steps? Do they seem to represent any social class or other groups? Do we see the fate of any of these people during the battle?

POETIC REALISM

Poetic realism was a film movement in France, primarily during the 1930s. I believe the most important point to address initially is the name itself. While this type of film has the term "realism" in its name and Italian neorealism comes close behind it as World War II ends, the two couldn't be more different. Indeed, many viewers will find a poetic realism film to be very stylized, very studio-bound, very artistic. In other words, very misnamed. When you think of poetic realism, think of the *poetic* part.

So this is not neorealism and these films do not look like documentaries. What stands out to me is the mood of the films and the look they often share. Not all poetic realism films look alike. They are much more diverse than some other movements. However, the mood in many of them dominates all else. These films are sad, brooding, hopeless. Often times, characters in a poetic realist film are trapped or doomed in some way. Like drowning victims, the last thing they cling to in hopes of salvation, is love. But ultimately, even this will fail. In fact, falling in love is often Fate's last cruel jest. Love just twists the knife in a bit deeper before the end.

If that sounds terribly depressing, it can be. However, it seems extremely appropriate for the period leading up to the Nazi domination of France, indeed all of Europe.

I think what really saves these films is that they are absolutely gorgeous! The overall atmosphere of many poetic realist films is shadowy, dark, brooding. Scenes are often shot in rich shadow or foggy, wet streets. Inside, directors seem to hang on objects that have special significance to the story: a broken

mirror, a lover's teddy bear, a bouquet of flowers. Characters are sad, disillusioned. Jean Gabin (the French version of Humphrey Bogart, I suppose) is often in these films. He wears a jaded, cynical shell, but his eyes are wonderful. Look in his eyes and it is clear the exterior is just for show. Underneath, he is lost and in pain, looking for salvation.

Legendary French film star, Jean Gabin (here in *The Grand Illusion*). For decades, he embodied the sad but jaded, world-weary Common Man.

World Pictures Corporation/Photofest

JEAN RENOIR

As I have said, the filmmakers of the poetic realism movement are not all cut from the same pattern—their films do not all have the same look. One of the directors often singled out in this type of film is **Jean Renoir**. Renoir is considered by many film authorities to be the absolute best filmmaker in the history of cinema (although those who love Orson Welles are sure to take offense). Perhaps a half-dozen of his films have been praised as masterworks. Two, **The Grand Illusion** (1937) and **The Rules of the Game** (1939) are widely considered to be among the very greatest films ever made.

A detailed analysis of *The Grand Illusion* follows, but mention of *The Rules of the Game* may illustrate how Renoir falls into the poetic realism movement. Set on a luxurious estate, the film studies class, especially contrasting the working class (represented by the servants at the manner) and the aristocracy (the owner and his guests). We see how brutal humanity can be, rich or poor. We see human frailty: our mistakes, our anger, our pride—we see it all. Renoir even plays a character in his own film, and gives himself a line that will stick with you for years. As the world begins to unravel and humanity's evils are exposed, Renoir's character sadly explains that "Everyone has his reasons." Renoir was a realist—he understood all of man's failures and even cruelty. And loved the world despite all that.

And something you realize while watching *The Rules of the Game* is that we are witnessing the final days of the aristocratic class. French, German, Russian—whatever—is dying and fading away. Renoir captures this same feeling in his war film *The Grand Illusion* as well.

MARCEL CARNÉ

While not regarded with the same acclaim as Renoir, **Marcel Carné** is perhaps the most artistic director of that era. His are the deepest shadows. His are the most lost and hopeless of characters. A prime example, *Port of Shadows* (1938), is the brooding story of an army deserter, who is about to escape and begin a new life, but love spells his doom. Some French politicians of the time criticized the film saying it was too fatalistic and depressing to represent the French people. Some

government officials even blustered, "If we lose this war, it will be because of *Port of Shadows!*" I've heard of a lot of things blamed for causing wars, but I think this is the first time I know of a movie being blamed for a military defeat.

CHILDREN OF PARADISE (1945)

First a note about the name of the film. In French theater, the upper levels of the house were referred to as "heaven" or "paradise" because the seats were so high up. So the title is a theater reference to "the cheap seats" or "nose-bleed section," if you will. Here are the common folk, the poor, and poorly-educated. But to these ordinary viewers, up in the cheap seats, the film was dedicated.

While *Children of Paradise* was made during the war and released more than six years after most of the influential films of the poetic realism movement had been made, this film still carries the same sad melancholy seen in films from the previous decade. It is essentially a historical fiction, featuring actual figures from the mid-19th century: Jean-Gaspard Deburau was an extremely well-known mime (in the film the character is called Baptiste—the real man's stage name). Frédérick Lemaître was a highly regarded actor. Pierre Lacenaire was a notorious French murderer—and poet. He'd be executed at the age of 32. Compte Edouard was fictional, but based on a real statesman, the Duc de Morny.

The Boulevard of Crime was a real place and Carné reproduces it in such amazing detail that one imagines that students of French history might look at the film to learn what the place was like. It was the most elaborate and expensive film set of the era. And a major storm destroyed it. The elements were just the beginning of the challenges in the making of this masterpiece.

Carné's production was under Vichy control. Basically, this meant that *Children of Paradise* was under the scrutiny of Vichy censors and Nazi censors as well. The director was forced to cast certain roles in the film with German sympathizers and collaborators. Ironically, those collaborators might very well find themselves working alongside members of the French underground! Jews were strictly forbidden from holding any job in the film industry, but a number of cases have been documented of Jews not only

The boulevard of crime—the grand world of Carné's *Children of Paradise* (1945). Destroyed by storms during production, it helps us understand why this film came to be called "the French Gone with the Wind."

working on the film, but being hidden by Carné and his friends throughout the production.[21] When the liberation began, the tables turned. Suddenly, it was the collaborators who were in trouble. In one case, an actor in a significant role was sentenced to be executed by the French. His part in the film fades quite abruptly. As for the actor, he turned up in Argentina.

The resulting film was worth all of the heartache. It has been called "the French *Gone with the Wind*" and still appears on every list of great films. Beautiful and yet sad, it goes with the era and with the film movement. *Children of Paradise* is a unique and special experience—one you need to have for yourself.

If all films were filled with the melancholy and gloom of poetic realism, it would become overwhelming. But included along with all the action pictures and musicals and comedies, these come like a cool, quiet, foggy morning.

---

[21] Some historians have estimated that prior to the war; roughly one-third of the French film industry was Jewish. Try to imagine the chaos if a major industry had one-third of its personnel eliminated almost overnight!

THE GRAND ILLUSION

Jean Renoir is often called the greatest filmmaker in the history of French cinema and two of his films *The Rules of the Game* (1939) and *The Grand Illusion* (1937) are inevitable titles on any Best Films list. However, it is never impressive cinematography that moves us, but portraits of wonderful characters. His film *The Grand Illusion* presents us with a whole group of well-defined people and relationships—and through them, Renoir brings us a profound view of the world and our place in it.

Perhaps the most important point to make regarding *The Grand Illusion* is to remind viewers what it is <u>not</u>. This is not a war film. It is not a POW film (at least in the general sense). It is a film about humanity and especially about human relationships. The war and the prisons are only the backdrops for a story about people who have been thrown together and how they mesh (and sometimes crash) together.

There are no dramatic battle scenes. Indeed, there was no budget for such action footage, but as is so often the case, the limits imposed are an advantage to a good director.[22] The film begins with a French squad room and a quick introduction of two of the central characters, Maréchal and de Boeldieu. We do not see their doomed mission or the dramatic dogfight that must have taken place. We just jump directly to a German squad room that looks almost exactly like the French one. The one real difference is in the figure of the fighter pilot, von Rauffenstein. His formality. His aristocratic bearing. Later, this

will become an important theme, but even in these opening shots of the film, he is extremely rigid—both physically and socially. Apart from him, the German soldiers throughout the film do not carry the sort of bombastic, maniacal quality of so many stereotypical movie German soldiers. They are human and are just as kind and courteous as their counterparts. In fact, we even see one German offer to cut Maréchal's meat—and their similarities (they are both mechanics) outweigh their differences.

The camaraderie is short-lived. A memorial wreath is brought in and we are reminded of the sad events that brought these men together. Guards arrive to take custody of the Frenchmen and it is as if the war resumes.

THE CAMP AT HALLBACH

The prisoners now arrive at Camp Hallbach, where we will get to know each of them and observe the relationships that develop. Indeed, one of the greatest things about *The Grand Illusion* is that the characters portrayed seem to become such real and natural people. Before the new prisoners are even shown to their quarters, we witness an amazing amount of human activity. Veteran prisoners try to warn the new men that their possessions are about to be taken. A British soldier stomps on his watch, breaking it rather than see it taken by a guard. De Boeldieu is indignant at being searched (and even here, we begin to see he doesn't want to be touched, physically or

---

[22] It is worth pointing out that in this, Jean Renoir and Orson Welles are much alike. Each of these great filmmakers frequently confronted financial problems. Granted, every person does—every business does—but in the cases of these two directors, I think the extreme financial challenges help to show just how ahead of their time they were.

emotionally). One prisoner's package from home has been opened and ruined while another's (Rosenthal) is carefully delivered (clearly, one needs to know who to bribe). And in a brief scene that is almost ignored, the German guards are shown eating even less than the prisoners. This little artificial community is a place full of activity and life.

Once settled into the prisoners' barracks, the newcomers (and the film audience) begin to get to know the men there. An actor named Cartier is constantly cutting up. He always has some sort of joke or song to insert into the conversation. Honestly, he may annoy us, but he's like a real person. Another character who stands out is a French Jew, Rosenthal, who is well-to-do and his packages from home are practically national holidays. He shares his bounty with his comrades and one of his cohorts even admits that he eats better in this POW camp than at any other time in his life. But Rosenthal's generosity seems based equally on friendly compassion and pride as well. We can see that he has a generous spirit, but also that this is his way of displaying his wealth and also one of his methods of defending himself against the inevitable anti-Semitism. Much like a real person, you may like Rosenthal or dislike him—what might stand out to you most may be kindness or pride. Either way, he is one of the most realistic, natural characters you are likely to see in a film.

There is an escape plan—there always has to be an escape plan. But a tunnel in a POW camp is a cliché. Remember, this isn't a war film and it isn't a POW film. This escape tunnel doesn't matter and indeed will never be used. It is a tool, a vehicle, which shows the audience more about the people. We see the prisoners working together—rich, poor, Jew, they all play their parts. Indeed, they seem almost like children playing at prison escape. Only when one of the prisoners learns that someone from another barrack has been killed trying to do the same thing is there pause to consider if they really even want to do this.

Throughout this section of the film there is a strong sense of play. The prisoners "hide" the dirt from their tunnel in the garden, with a complete lack of subtlety. One of our protagonists, Maréchal, is thrown in solitary confinement, but proves that he can break out when he wants, almost like a child barred from recess. And the prisoners gain permission from their jailors to hold a play.

While it may seem like a fairly insignificant scene, the play does several things. We see the Germans and the French, all as simple human beings. They enjoy the diversion of the play. They all dream of the magic of the women missing from their lives. It is only when we suddenly learn of a seemingly important military victory that the sides are shorn apart. The play is over and *the play* is over as well.

And within a day or two that important military victory has bounced back and forth like some sort of diabolical ping pong ball until we realize it is meaningless. Victory is an illusion. *A Grand Illusion.*

Another futility. Another illusion. The tunnel is almost ready and our little band is transferred. The exiting prisoners try desperately to tell the new ones about the tunnel, but language frustrates them (languages in this film are critical). Their efforts have been useless. And now they move on to another camp—and a darker act in the drama.

CASTLE WINTERSBORN

The main characters are moved to a POW camp at the cliff-side castle of Wintersborn. The castle is dark and cold. You can feel the change to the tone of the whole film. After his absence at the more casual camp at Hallbach, von Rauffenstein reappears here—a catastrophic injury has locked him permanently in a neck and back brace (and given him a promotion to go with it). He is now the commandant here and takes little time in warning the new prisoners not to attempt to escape from this place.

He resumes his friendship with fellow aristocrat, de Boeldieu, but things have changed. De Boeldieu has come to care about his comrades and to realize that his class is a dying breed. In contrast, von Rouffenstein has become more stiff (not just physically, but mentally). Like his last pair of dress gloves, he stubbornly refuses to try to change who he is. The difference may seem subtle to modern viewers, but it is a dramatic change in personalities that will bring on a collision—indeed the climax of the story.

Remember how important the use of various languages is throughout the film? Remember that English is used when the two aristocrats talk between themselves? They use it again here. And ultimately, one man is able to rise above his station, while one is trapped—doomed to live out his days as a last member of his vanishing class. Remember, to Renoir, the station that matters is not an economic or social one—it is nobility. De Boeldieu achieves it.

ILLUSIONS

I become too long-winded when discussing a film that fascinates me. However, how I need to conclude is to consider the title. Students sometimes ask, "So just what *is* the illusion?" There are several aren't there? In an early version of the script, the prisoners promise to meet at a restaurant on New Year's Eve when the war is over. That version of the story ends with a reserved table on New Year's Eve—empty. Maréchel promises Elsa that after the war, he will return. Will he? And most important, as the film ends, Maréchel tells Rosenthal they must continue fighting so they end it and there will be no more wars. Really? They called the First World War, *The War to End All Wars*. Now we number them. The very last words of the film acknowledge that national borders are random lines on a map and no one even agrees on where they really lie in a snowy field. If anyone asks you, "So what is the grand illusion?" would you reply, "Which one?"

GIVE ME YOUR FEEDBACK:
THE GRAND ILLUSION

1. Name at least three "Illusions" that the title might be referring to:

2. Do you think Maréchel ever came back to the farm woman and her daughter?

3. The time of the aristocracy is passing. Both von Rauffenstein and de Boeldieu see it. How does each confront that change?

ITALIAN NEOREALISM

BEFORE THE NEOREALIST MOVEMENT

Lavish Italian spectacle films, like *Quo Vadis?* (1924) had been extremely successful in the silent era, but by the 1930s, Italy was making few films and what was made certainly didn't garner any attention. The films of this period were often light-weight comedies—mostly about the trivial and silly problems of the rich. These pictures gained their own nickname—and not a complimentary one. They were called "**white telephone**" films, named for the fact that all the regular folks had black phones. The only person with a white telephone was someone so rich that they had nothing else to waste their money upon! Today we might nickname such films "Champagne and caviar comedies" or something like that. They were not treated seriously. The audience could not relate to what they saw on screen any more than I can really understand what it's like to be a billionaire.

When Benito Mussolini took total power in 1925, the role of cinema changed in Italy.[23] This might seem illogical to some, since Mussolini was known as a fascist and Vladimir Lenin was a communist, but the Italian took many of his political cues from the Soviet leader. To Lenin, "Film is the most important art," so it was valued the same way by Mussolini. And for the same reason—it was an extremely powerful propaganda tool. As early as 1924, Mussolini was using cinema as a "cultural education tool" and within a decade, film production was totally controlled by the government.

So Italians of that era primarily knew of two types of cinema: the silly fluff of the "white telephone" style and government-controlled propaganda. Imagine the frustration you might feel in this circumstance, realizing *both* types were lies intended to delude people!

NEOREALISM

So the 1930s and early 1940s were a time of tremendous frustration for many Italian film viewers, especially those who held opposing political views. I can even imagine people sitting in the dark watching those films, angrily telling themselves that a new kind of film needed to be made. Well, in 1943 everything came to a head. The Allies invaded in southern Italy and Mussolini was ousted by his own fascist party. The conflict wasn't over by any means, but government control of cinema began to slip. The result was a dramatically different type of film. It quickly became known as "the new realism" or "**neorealism**."

Try to appreciate how raw and fresh these films must have seemed to the Italian audience—and to the world at large. The very first neorealist film to gain international attention, called *Rome, Open City* (or simply *Open City* (1945) chronicled the violence

---

[23] Mussolini actually ran the country as its constitutionally elected Prime Minster starting in 1922, but really became Italy's dictator about three years later.

that erupted in Rome during the clash between occupying Nazis and Italian resistance fighters.[24] It was shot in the streets. Film stock was in short supply and of poor quality. The result was a film that looked like news reels of the time, not a fiction film. Some viewers thought they were watching a documentary.

The film is a wonderful example of the key elements of Italian neorealism. These films avoid overly-contrived, highly-scripted stories and they are about ordinary people in real life situations. No white telephones here! No rich celebrities! In fact, neorealism would be well-known for its refusal to cast experienced professional actors at all, or in mixing unknown professionals and non-professionals. Also, while these films may not offer direct criticisms of Italian government and society as a whole, the filmmakers were almost all leftists (socialists, communists, etc.) and their films implicitly carry the message that fascism has failed and that the country needs a new political direction.

It is also critical to pose a few questions about the movement here as well. First, I might ask you to consider the casting of performers in neorealist films. *What really is a non-professional actor?* Is this simply a term for anyone who has never been in a film before? Is it a person who has had no training as an actor? Is it a person who has a "regular day job," such as being a construction worker? *Does it really make a difference?* If I cast a construction worker in a leading role in my new film, don't I then spend time "coaching" him on how to act? Maybe you disagree, but it seems to me that I am training him as an actor on the job. The Italian neorealist filmmakers insisted that they were rejecting the kind of highly-scripted, contrived stories that Hollywood was well-known for, but their own films are *not* documentaries about real events. They are scripted and they are indeed fiction—even though they look natural. Are the writers and directors of this movement trying to give us some sort of unmanipulated, totally honest Truth? If so, why script out a story line and hire actors (of

whatever sort) to play these characters? Listen to the music in a film like *Shoeshine* (1946) or *Bicycle Thieves* (1948). Is this objective, or is it a manipulation of the audience, leading us to feel sorry for the characters' sad situations? Perhaps I am being harsh here, but I want to make a point. These films seem very honest and natural, but they are manipulated just as surely as those fascist propaganda films were. The filmmakers' goal may have been to show us real life as it existed outside the movie theater, but are they simply better (remarkably better) storytellers than their predecessors?

GLOBAL INFLUENCE

The neorealist movement had burned out in Italy by about 1952. Italians in general were taking a more optimistic view of the future and one official even called neorealism, "dirty laundry that shouldn't be washed and hung to dry in the open."

But to this day, the brief neorealist movement is known as Italian cinema's Golden Age and a wide variety of filmmakers around the world were inspired by its grass-roots simplicity. The directors **Fellini** and **Antonioni** are descendants of neorealism. Both of these legendary *auteurs* learned their film craft participating in the movement.

Many third world nations owe their cinema in some part to neorealism. Simple equipment, stories that are based on ordinary life, low budget productions—the connection is obvious. If you were living in an underdeveloped nation and dreamed of making films, this movement would immediately inspire you. **Satyajit Ray** of India would become one of the world's most highly regarded directors. **Ousmane Sembène** is often referred to as the Father of African Cinema. You will easily see the influence of Italian neorealism in the films of both men.

Neorealism did not last long officially, but you see it in a large portion of the films produced ever since— even new films you might see today.

---

[24] A 1943 film, *Obsession*, is recognized today as an even earlier neorealist film, but it was an illegal adaptation of *The Postman Always Rings Twice*, which violated the copyright of the original work and could not be screened outside Italy until 1976.

THE BICYCLE THIEF/ BICYCLE THIEVES (1948)

Note: the common American title of the film is *The Bicycle Thief*, however the correct translation is *Bicycle Thieves*. A minor change like this is often insignificant, but in this case, it changes the meaning of the entire film. Here we will use *Bicycle Thieves*, but I catch myself in lectures using the other title—I'm just as guilty as the next person. The important thing here is to be aware of the significance of this change.

This is the story of a man in post-World War Two Italy searching for his stolen bicycle. *Not much of a premise.* Oh, and without his bicycle, he will lose his job. *Well, that at least makes it more significant.* And without the job, his family's welfare is in serious jeopardy. *Even now, this doesn't sound like much of a film plot.*

But even decades after its release, this is still considered to be one of the greatest films ever made. So the fascination of this film must not be in just the plot. It's just such a simple film. No special effects. No great Hollywood star in the leading role. Good grief—no one even dies! But despite what appears to be a film no one would care about, *Bicycle Thieves* continues to work well, decades after it was made, even for an audience that is literally (and figuratively) on the other side of the world.

So take a closer look at the film to see what catches your attention and decide why it still works for us today.

THE ENVIRONMENT

The first thing you will notice as the film begins is the environment. Bare dirt, bombed out buildings, rubble. There is no running water. The townswomen are drawing water with buckets from a communal well, just as if this were two thousand years ago. Sometimes a good film can activate senses a viewer doesn't normally use in a film—here I can feel the rust and dirt on every surface. I inhale the dust. You almost do not notice that the film is in black and white—there are no colors anyway. No plants.

We are introduced to the main characters, the Ricci family, who are as disheveled and hopeless as the city around them. We are shown in the very first moments of the film that work is a rare commodity and that a citizen might wait for months or even years to get a job. Antonio Ricci (Lamberto Maggiorani) is given a job. But he must have a bicycle from his very first day of training.

The one way to make this depressing situation even worse is to offer a glimmer of hope—just a vague promise that things might get better. And then dash even that hope to pieces.

The Ricci home is no better than the city around it. The apartment is cramped and claustrophobic. You feel as if you could reach out and touch walls on either side of the room. The place is bare. The only pictures on the wall are photographs of relatives (which no one would buy) and to make it even more gloomy, one of those has a black sash, indicating that the person has died. The wife, Maria, finds a solution to their immediate need—to get their bicycle out of hock. But the solution? Sell all their sheets. That's how thin their options have become. And note the way Maria's voice breaks when she tells her husband they can sleep without sheets!

One of the most powerful scenes in the film—and one you should give special attention—is at the government pawn shop (sorry, I don't know what else to call it). We see the Riccis sell their sheets (which had probably been a prized possession for a poor family) and as Antonio claims his bicycle, he watches an employee add their sheets to an absolutely huge rack of sheets. It is a mountain! And we suddenly realize that it has a meaning. It isn't just the Ricci family that is in financial despair—*everyone* has hocked their sheets.

There is no relief. On his very first day of work, Antonio has his bicycle stolen. By this point, we realize this isn't just the theft of a bike. It endangers this family's very survival. Antonio frantically chases the young man, but is delayed by the thief's friends. The premise here is so simple it almost seems silly. Ricci spends the rest of the film trying to get his bicycle back, only to be frustrated at every turn. The thief meets briefly with an old man, but the old man is so uncooperative that you just want to punch him! Antonio and his young son, Bruno (an amazing performance by Enzo Staiola) find the thief and follow him to his building. They even get the police. For their efforts, the victim is almost beaten by the thief's neighbors and the police simply advise him to give up.

We watch helplessly as Antonio's frustration and panic rise to the breaking point. Finally, he does what I think we all knew he would do eventually. He sends little Bruno away and tries to steal a bicycle himself.

It is worth returning to the title of the film for a moment. Yes, the bicycle thief (singular) is the young man who stole Ricci's means of making a living. However, the correct title is *Bicycle Thieves*. So who are the thieves (plural)? Some of my students quickly respond that the young thief is not alone. That his friend the old man, his neighborhood allies and even his family are all in it together. They are *all* bicycle thieves. But those students only partly right, aren't they. Antonio Ricci is a decent man and a wonderful father, yet he too becomes a bicycle thief. In fact, any of us—all of us just might become bicycle thieves too, given the right (or should that be "wrong") circumstances! Maybe the film even makes us remember an old expression, "There, but for the grace of God, go I."

Despite its simplicity, many viewers find *Bicycle Thieves* to be one of the most depressing and hopeless of films. It is easy to agree. Fate seems to take a particular glee in ruining Ricci's life and mocking him in every way imaginable. The only glimmer of real hope I am left with is given to us by the little boy, Bruno. As they walk away from the entire horrible adventure, he takes his father's hand. And I am reminded that Antonio and his wonderful family still live and will wake up again tomorrow and struggle and survive. And the next day. Sometimes you fight, even when no one notices.

Where there's life there's hope?

GIVE ME YOUR FEEDBACK:
BICYCLE THIEVES

1. *Bicycle Thieves* uses a combination of professional and non-professional actors. Based on the character portrayals in the film, do you think their performances are different in any way? Do you think this neorealist habit mattered?

2. The film says almost nothing about government—nothing about the local leadership and nothing about any particular government services. Despite this, do you think *Bicycle Thieves* carries an unspoken criticism about a government that is corrupt or incompetent?

3. This film looks like a non-fiction, documentary about real conditions in a real city, but it is not. It is a made up fiction film. What elements of the film do you notice that are manipulated and set up by the filmmakers to create the right feelings for an audience?

JAPANESE CINEMA

Given its distance from the film capitals of Europe and the United States, it may surprise some to learn that Japan has one of the oldest and best-developed film industries in the world. Touring cameramen came to Japan in the late 1890s and by 1900 Japanese filmmakers were making that country's first cinema. There were many Japanese silent films, some of which have survived and can still be viewed and studied today. The Japanese cinema benefited from film's close relationship to a strong live performance tradition in that country. Films have been compared with *kubaki* and *bunraku* (traditional puppet theater). Silent Japanese films were often accompanied by a *benshi*, a narrator who stood beside the screen and commented on the images on screen. Some films were even accompanied by live music, as was done in the West.

TWO MASTERS

During the silent era, the first two Japanese master directors, **Kenji Mizoguchi** and **Yasujirō Ozu**, emerged and continue to stand high in the eyes of critics world-wide. While many of the silent films of each director are now lost, what can still be seen reveals traits—as if each filmmaker leaves a signature that can be recognized by a student of cinema. With Mizoguchi, one often confronts human pain and suffering with amazing compassion. His later films focus upon women's lives and even the notion of suffrage. Visually, he leaves a calling-card as well. Mizoguchi films often make use of a very complex cinematic technique that one might call "One scene—one shot." Through meticulous preparation,

he designs an entire scene so it does not need to be cut into pieces—it plays out as a very natural, uninterrupted experience for the viewer.

Ozu also drew his inspiration from the ordinary and the simple. His films are about family. The relationships between different generations. The Common Man's daily life and little struggles. In a typical Ozu film, the first thing one is likely to notice is the camera placement: it is often placed on the floor. It is as if the viewer is sitting on a tatami mat right in the middle of the family and their lives. Also noteworthy is the fact that this director is likely to skip pieces of his story—even important ones. The story may be building up to a wedding celebration, but the filmmaker jumps past it, not even showing the event. It is as if Ozu removed a major event and left behind a series of ellipses (…) to mark its passing.

In their later years, following World War II, both Mizoguchi and Ozu were considered old fashioned and out-of-date in their own country. However, in the West, these two directors would become revered as two of the three great film masters to come from Japan. The third would be Akira Kurosawa.

THE THIRD MASTER: AKIRA KUROSAWA

Akira Kurosawa is the best-known and highly regarded director in Japanese film history. Especially in the West, he is without equal. The 1950s are considered to be The Golden Age of Japanese Cinema and Kurosawa really led the way (at least as far as

Western audiences were concerned). His 1950 film *Rashomon* won both the Golden Lion at the Venice Film Festival and was the Best Foreign Film at the Academy Awards. It put Japan on the cinema map and along the way, made Toshiro Mifune into a major international film star. Kurosawa's 1954 epic *Seven Samurai* is a more popular film, but in my opinion, there are critical elements in *Rashomon* that warrant special attention in an upcoming essay.

Even a quick viewing of their films easily shows that Kurosawa's technical style is profoundly different from that of Ozu and Mizoguchi. Words like "bold" and "disruptive" are used to describe his style. Kurosawa's films have even been compared with a whirlwind—chaotic and in constant motion. Rather than use a smooth zoom to get closer to a player, he might cut together a series of rough shots, as if the camera is jumping or lunging at the subject. He uses sound and specifically music more deliberately than most other directors (even modern ones). He might play a beautiful piece by Mozart to accompany a sword fight. At one point in a violent battle in *Seven Samurai*, chirping birds are heard in the background.

Several major themes are repeated in many Kurosawa films. He favors a strong, central protagonist who must fight against the odds and find his own way. Some critics theorize that their defeat in World War II made many Japanese stop believing in their government, even in their Emperor. Kurosawa's response seems to be the creation of individual heroes, who must make their own way in life—even through pain. In *Ikiru* (1952)—a modern story about the life of a common, seemingly unimportant office worker—we see the uplifting story of a man who stands up and creates a legacy. The master/apprentice relationship is explored frequently as in his very first film, *Sanshiro Sugata* and his very last, *Madadayo.*

The last theme I wish to mention here is a very dark one. In the works of Kurosawa, especially in his later ones, he sees a world that revolves in a continual spiral of violence. Ultimately, there is no way out. No way to break the cycle. Being a hero or a teacher doesn't matter. The violent world will continue to churn—and in that repetition of violence, Kurosawa sees the world as a kind of hell.

THE JAPANESE NEW WAVE

Times change. Society changes. And since cinema is not made inside some sort of magic bubble, the films made by a society change as well. Cinema in 1960s and 1970s Japan was a form of rebellion. A group of New Wave directors challenged the many traditions and rules that governed Japanese society.

Let's take just one example here. **Nagisa Oshima**. In films like *Death by Hanging* (1968) and the notorious *In the Realm of the Senses* (1976), Oshima questions social constraint and deconstructs his culture's traditional doctrines. For the Japanese New Wave, film is a weapon, used to question and even condemn social norms.

HAYAO MIYAZAKI: THE JAPANESE DISNEY

From the very start, I have had to completely eliminate various types of films from our discussion; there are no documentaries, almost no avant-garde, and no animated films. If I were to break my own rule just once, I would discuss the animation filmmaker **Hayao Miyazaki**. I would argue Miyazaki is more highly regarded and will be better remembered than some of the great live-action directors mentioned above. He is the Japanese Walt Disney.

However, if I begin talking about Miyazaki, I must then discuss anime. And if I discuss anime, I would have no choice, but to examine *Grave of the Fireflies* (1988). And I just don't have the heart to do that.

Obviously, my fascination with Japanese cinema has no bounds. But it seems to me that the films of this country include something for anyone to love. Anime films like *Ghost in the Shell* thrill the eye and send the imagination soaring as well. Suspense and thrills are available for any sensibility—from the shadowy legends (in some of the most glorious photography ever) in *Kuroneko* (1968) to the more modern approach offered by *Dark Water* (2002). Samurai films like *Twilight Samurai* (2002) keep the traditional *jidaigeki* alive and spin it as a very human conflict between social duty and love of family. And when none of these appeal, there's always Godzilla.

RASHOMON (1950)

Today, years after his death, Akira Kurosawa is still considered to be the most important Japanese director in the history of world cinema. *Rashomon* won the prestigious Golden Lion at the Venice Film Festival. It was the film that put him on the map internationally. But while some films go out of fashion and lose their edge, *Rashomon* probably speaks to our sensibilities more effectively today than when it was first seen.

Rashomon (1950) is a *jidaigeki*, a period drama based on two short stories about the samurai era. A priest and a woodcutter are joined by a (rather cynical, bitter) commoner, as they hide under the Rashomon gate to avoid a rainstorm. To kill time, the priest and the woodcutter tell the peasant about a shocking incident that happed nearby. The key to the film is that this story is told in four different versions, from four different perspectives. A bandit encountered a samurai and his wife in the woods, but just what happened depends on who is telling the story. The samurai may have been a brave warrior killed in battle, or he may have been a heartless coward. The beautiful young woman may have been raped, or she may have willingly sided with the bandit against her husband. Four different versions of the story—and different subjective perspectives. Who is telling the truth? The audience desires closure and solution.

They do not get it. The film viewer realizes in the end that no one is telling the truth. That all of the characters see only through their own perspectives and biases. There is, in fact, no Objective Truth. And that's the point of the movie.

It's been said before: a great film should be seen more than once. The audience of *Rashomon* will gain a great deal with one viewing. But it will be mostly about the plot and the theme of the film—that all the stories are subjective and that there is ultimately *no* absolute truth to be found. A second viewing will reveal more and, I think, give the viewer more to appreciate about the film.

If you are attempting that second viewing and are trying to find "a way in" to discover more about the film, it is sometimes useful to take notes as you watch. Do not worry about saying something "deep" or significant—just jot down the things that stand out for you.

For example, as *Rashomon* opens, we see its framing story—the men gathered at the gate waiting out the rainstorm and telling various parts of the incident in the grove. I note the condition of the gate. It was once strong and beautiful, but is nothing but a skeleton now—a rotting corpse. The peasant tears off boards to build a fire. We are even told there may be dead bodies tossed aside here, like so much rubbish. The clothing of the three men is much the same. This isn't the Golden Age of the Samurai and these aren't nobles. They are in rags, they are impoverished. The appearance of both the gate and the men tell us this is a dying culture, a sad place with no direction or meaning.

I think I first begin to appreciate the very production values of the film as the woodcutter's story begins. Kurosawa impresses me as a filmmaker just as much in the early scenes of *Rashomon* as he will with the grand costumes and sets of *Ran*. This is a bare-bones production, perhaps even a film a student could attempt without a meaningful budget. Kurosawa does an amazing amount filmically with very little. How does the woodcutter's story begin?

We notice the moving camera, the music, the changing shot choices as the character walks through the woods. We are even treated to some beautiful photographic moments: the woodcutter crossing a bridge (shot from below), the sun glinting between the leaves of the trees. We can just feel the quiet and the enclosed feeling of these woods. It's hot. There is very little breeze and we can hear the insects buzzing in the shadows. We feel the sweat drip down the character's neck.

As much as anything, I have the feeling that the woodcutter is very small and insignificant. Kurosawa became well-known for using actors frequently. Takashi Shimura, who plays the woodcutter, was in 21 Kurosawa films. He is a perfect type for many of his roles—he seems small, powerless, weak. As the woodcutter, he is that unimportant fellow you walk past and don't even really see. As an actor, he uses this persona as a tool—as a mask, and the woodcutter does much the same. He is unassuming and meek. Another character in the story would pass him by without even noticing him. His first story (there will be two) serves to bring us to the site of the incident and gives us a few of the clues left there. I feel almost like I am watching a typical American detective film and this is my first look at the crime scene.

Next, the priest relates his observations, but notice that it is not a full-fledged telling of the incident. The priest didn't really see much of the event—but, significantly, he is a witness to all that surrounds the incident. Played by another Kurosawa regular, Minoru Chiaki, I get a strong sense of the man's mood. He probably feels that his demeanor displays humility and piety, but to me he seems slow, somber, even depressed. And always he is the *observer*. Consider the way that he seems to pay close attention to the world around him and its people. How often is he shown in the background of a scene—*just watching*? Some critics have suggested that the priest represents Kurosawa's own viewpoint on the subject matter. He is the thoughtful, contemplative one. But no matter how he tries to distance himself from the world around him, he is trapped by it. This event in particular haunts him—and hurts him.

If Takahashi would become a legend as Kurosawa's common man, Toshiro Mifune was his typhoon. As the bandit, Tajōmaru, Mifune is manic, insane, even

comical. In his story, I am more captivated by the movements of the actors, not the camerawork. But even in his own version of events, Tajōmaru is graceless and erratic. He claims his duel with the samurai was something impressive, but he must have been watching a different fight than I was![25] The bandit and the samurai are both thugs—and they stab the dirt more often than their opponents.

As the saying goes, things now start to get interesting. In a powerful performance by legendary actress Machiko Kyō, the wife's story shows us a very different personality than we see elsewhere. She faints, she weeps, she moans about how weak and useless she is. The early stories portray her as an object for the men to use and fight over, but here she tries to flaunt it. Their perception of her is a tool she uses. But even as she insists on her faithfulness and support of her husband, I begin to see through the farce—maybe it's here that I notice the refrains of "Bolero" in the music score.

The most shocking comparison is made between the woman's story and the husband's (told through a medium). The stories of the husband and the wife are the most directly linked and what we see brings the film to another level. The woman's story is full of her expected emotions and reactions, but note that I call them the *expected* emotions. We can see through them, even in her own version. They are the things a female of this period is *supposed* to do and say, but even here we can tell they are not genuine. To confirm this, Kurosawa follows her tale with that of her husband. Her tears are false. Her protestations are a mask. But now we get to see what is underneath. When you get past the expected—past the social standard—she hates both of them. She'd just as soon see them both dead. It's really rather frightening. She's full of hate. Indeed, she is more insane than the bandit.

The wife's only true emotion displayed is during the duel itself. She's gotten what she wanted and they are fighting. However, she's calculating what will happen to her in the aftermath—and she is afraid of what she sees. Now that she's manipulated them into this situation, there are no good outcomes for her (and even now she doesn't care at all about what happens to the men). Kurosawa is sometimes criticized for the portrayals of women in his films, but

---

[25] Toshiro Mifune also starred in the Kurosawa film *Sanjiru*. His swordsmanship was considered so exceptional that it has been shown in kendo manuals. Certainly, the swordfights in *Rashomon* will not appear in any kendo books!

Rashomon shows how incomplete these criticisms are. The wife is a fascinating—and frightening—character, indeed.[26]

So whether you find her to be a cunning, manipulative black widow or a woman held captive by her society, using the only sort of power at her disposal, the wife is the most dangerous of the characters. But ultimately, she is as doomed as the men.

The final story, the woodcutter's more truthful admission, is supposed to be the resolution of the film. It is supposed to reveal "what really happened," but does it? The viewer watches this tale with a greater sense of expectation—anticipating that all of the lies and subjectivity that have come before will now be rejected in favor of the Truth. It isn't. As we watch, the final story is shown to be a lie, just like the others.

Film historians correctly identify *Rashomon* as an extremely dark, pessimistic film. Indeed, the Japanese film industry originally feared to distribute it in the West, or submit it to award contests because they thought it was "too Japanese" and that Western audiences might not appreciate its cynical perspective. There is no Truth. Ultimately, there is no objective, accurate version of the story for Kurosawa or his audience to experience. Each story is told from someone's point of view and is colored with their perspectives and motives. And in the end, the film would say, none of us can ever know the world around us in some correct, honest way. There isn't one. *Rashomon* cannot end with the resolution

of a correct answer. Humans only experience Life subjectively. We can't step outside the game and see the world around us as if we have stopped being players and are suddenly referees. Honestly, if one thinks seriously about this film, its extreme cynicism becomes almost overwhelming. There is no Truth. Everyone has his or her own motives and perspectives and it isn't possible to escape that. And along with questioning the existence of Truth, can we really believe there is a Right or a Wrong? Is there Good and Evil? I'm no philosopher, but the way I see it, *Rashomon* paints a world in which there is no right and wrong answer to the question—what happened in the woods that day. And no one in the story is good or evil. Does the body of the film ultimately conclude that it is impossible for any of us to really *do good*? A dark story, indeed!

In the end, I am reminded of how disturbed the priest and woodcutter are over this story—obsessed with this one murder among many. But in a way, the cynicism of the incident in the grove goes hand-in-hand with the discovery of the baby. This particular murder bothered them in a profound way. It pierced their hearts. Perhaps it reminded them that a bandit, a noble samurai warrior and a beautiful woman were all equally human, equally stained. All of us wear masks and all of us lie. But if that is the real meaning of the incident in the grove, the discovery of the baby has restored hope for two of the men. The bitter peasant will never see it, but the priest and the woodcutter understand in the end.

---

[26] Another great example can be seen in *Ran*. One of the main characters, Lady Kaede, displays the ability to switch on and off her subservience and helplessness as if with a switch. I won't give anything away here, but note the scene when she notices an insect on the floor!

GIVE ME YOUR FEEDBACK:
RASHOMON

1. What does the wife see as possible outcomes for her? Depending on the result of the duel, what will happen to her?

2. Some critics believe the peasant represents the perspective of the audience. Do you agree with this assessment? What characteristics does the commoner pose that echo the viewer's point of view?

3. What examples did you notice of people watching events?

THE FRENCH NEW WAVE

In many cases, the various cinema movements we examine have a striking visual style that unites a variety of films from different directors—German expressionism, for example. Sometimes, there is a prevailing philosophy or world view that makes the films of the movement seem almost like siblings—my first thought is French poetic realism. However, with the French New Wave you will get very little of either of these important links. The films may look dramatically different and be made by directors with remarkably dissimilar philosophies.

What becomes clear with this New Wave is that it is best understood as a time period—even an environment—not films that have something in common on screen.

A time period—a context—maybe a convergence. The films being made in France in the 1950s were called The Tradition of Quality, but for young viewers of that era, "Tradition" implied an old, dusty predictability. To them, "Quality" implied film-makers resting on their impressive reputations and delivering nothing but "more of the same." A group of young film fans were quickly growing from being mere viewers to being critics and even started to publish in the cinema journals of the time. Welcomed and encouraged by film historians **André Bazin** and **Henri Langlois**, these young *cinephiles* (including François Truffaut, Éric Rohmer, and Jean Luc Godard) called ever more loudly for fresh, creative minds to be given the opportunity to make films. (And if these new filmmakers just happened to be themselves, so much the better, right?) Between roughly 1959–1964 a number of them got the chance—and film was changed dramatically.

I do not look at the films of the New Wave and see an abundance of similarities. These new filmmakers do have some important tendencies: they often exhibit a youthful spirit of rebellion, both in plot and production techniques. Often times, these films have very ambiguous endings. You are likely never to find nice satisfying closure to these films. These directors are, to one degree or another, very passionate about cinema—not just making it, but watching it and even talking about it. Frequently, you can see a French New Wave film that makes references to previous films (like *Citizen Kane*) or movie stars (like Bogart).

So what we see is an exciting variety in the films of this era. They break rules. They mock social norms. They celebrate the unusual. But each filmmaker does those things in different ways. **François Truffaut** is often fun-loving. His films are about youthful characters, their pranks and unconventional relationships. **Jean Luc Godard** seems to me to change quite dramatically during his long career. In early films like *Breathless*, he exhibits a rough, almost sloppy, technical style. In the late 1960s with social rebellion in the air, he makes a film like *Weekend*, which links capitalism with cannibalism. **Alain Resnais** (who was older—not one of those boys mentioned earlier) offers up extremely dreamy, almost hallucinogenic films like *Last Year at Marienbad* (1961). We wander around an old mansion contemplating the décor: the paintings, the frescos, the gardens. The guests visiting there seem to be in some sort of trance—and you will never be sure if they know each other or are strangers. You will never know if they were all here "Last year at Marienbad" or even if they are ghosts who haunt the place forever.

1964 is a pretty arbitrary end-date. Indeed, many of the New Wave directors continued their careers for decides after that. However, 1959–1964 is a window that includes the first feature films of some of the most exciting directors of that era. Many of their works will morph dramatically with the times and the social issues at stake. But a significant change had taken place. Films of the New Wave were often seen in small art house theaters and the patrons would talk about the films and what they meant afterward. In retrospect, it almost seems a bit like the cinema classes that would soon pop up on college campuses all over the world.

TRUFFAUT AND *THE 400 BLOWS*

François Truffaut is the most liked and accessible of the directors of the French New Wave. His films often exhibit a fun quality. They are frequently about free spirits who break the rules—but not in a vicious, hurtful way. And it is obvious Truffaut loves cinema. In this, he is like us and we embrace him for it. Once you've seen a few of his films, there will be images and ideas that you will take with you for years. Pleasant ones. In *Jules and Jim* we have a love triangle in which two young men are both in love with a beautiful girl. Rather than descending into some battle or having one of them cast out and rejected, the film celebrates the relationship of all three of them. It's fun, unconventional, maybe a bit mischievous. In *Day for Night*, Truffaut himself plays a director trying to make a movie (as if we needed to be reminded that this is a film, not reality, right?). There's a wonderful series of interviews with the stars of the film-within-a-film explaining what the film is about. Each of them believes the film is the story of *their* character and how the other characters affect them. It's funny as it dawns on us that each of these actors believe their own character (and thus they, themselves) are the star of the film! Discovering Truffaut, even after all this time, can be a wonderful experience. But he will forever be best-known for his very first picture, *The 400 Blows*, and it is a film mix of laughter and perhaps a few tears as well.[27]

THE 400 BLOWS (1959)

François Truffaut's first film is *The 400 Blows* (1959). Let's start with the name. The French title, *Les Quatre Cents Coups,* is an expression basically meaning to "raise hell." In 1959 America, someone didn't think it was a good idea to use "The H-Word" in a film title, so now we know it by a name no one confuses with any other title for anything else, but also one that no English-speaker understands. Probably the one thing that fans know better than anything else is that the film is autobiographical. Truffaut himself grew up neglected and rebellious. He cast a boy who looked something like him. As the years went by, he'd have the same actor play semi-autobiographical characters in other films. Ironically, as he grew older, the actor, Jean-Pierre Léaud, resisted the character Truffaut had created for him. But for all of that, the character he plays, Antoine Doinel, is someone we can all relate to on a variety of levels. Indeed, I believe that we can understand and appreciate him no matter what age we are, whether we think of ourselves as children or as parents—that is why the film remains wonderful. While some New Wave directors clearly do not care for the characters in their films—in some cases even dislike them—Truffaut loves this boy and understands him. And we do too.

As you watch the film, look for a progression of sorts. The film starts as a very amusing story of childhood rebellion. Our protagonist has a very insensitive teacher. He's the black sheep at home. Honestly, viewers almost think of this as being only the boy's point of view and that perhaps the objective reality of his life really isn't even that bad. He cuts school and goes on rather amusing adventures in town. He even has company—he shares his experience with a friend. Touches of the New Wave are introduced

---

[27] Yes, this is a Charlie Chaplin reference. *The Kid* begins with these words. I thought Truffaut would like it.

Truffaut and *The 400 Blows*   63

almost gently here: Antoine's love of movies, his lighthearted rebellion. But it's fun and harmless.

To me it is his plagiarism of Balzac that marks a turning point. For once, maybe for the first time in his life, a light goes on for young Antoine. It's as if for one precious moment, learning becomes meaningful to him personally—it isn't just some annoying exercise forced upon him. Why does he plagiarize Balzac? Is he trying to cheat? Is he rebelling against his teacher once again? No! The quote *means* something to him. When he uses Balzac's words as his own, he is not stealing them—he is *claiming* them! It could be the start of something. It could be the birth of a new Antoine Doinel—one that is beginning to learn.

But it is not to be. The film turns notably darker to me at this point. His connection with Balzac leads to a cheating charge and huge problems at school. Even at home, his "new leaf" leads only to another catastrophic failure. His altar to Balzac (indeed his altar to learning) literally goes up in flames. The moment for change is gone. The new Antoine is dead. And what is he left with?

Frankly, not much. His family situation is much worse than we expected. Family members who do not trust him—do not even love him. A father who is weak and disrespected (not even his biological father, but a stepfather, who is understanding and likable enough at times, but no one takes him seriously). Antoine quits school and attempts to steal a typewriter from his stepfather's office.

He doesn't even do this right. He is arrested trying to put back the typewriter. Fed up, his parents let him be put in jail and seeing this 14-year-old boy sitting in a cold cell next to winos and prostitutes is truly a disturbing image. Gone are the carefree days of giving teacher the slip and sneaking into a movie!

It isn't fun and games anymore. As *The 400 Blows* progresses, Antoine moves from silly antics to jail. Here he is being fingerprinted.

Here we arrive at the final chapter of this Antoine Doinel story. He is placed in a residential facility and the professionals try to learn a bit about him—what makes him tick, but it's too late. We probably understand him better than they ever will. Even here, he runs away.

This last escape is the most tragic for us. We know where he is going and sadly we know what he will discover when he gets there. As he once promised, he escapes to the sea. But as he runs through the water, he slows and stops. It has just hit him. There is no Grand New Beginning here—it is just a Dead End. He turns and Truffaut gives us that shocking freeze frame of the boy looking at us (shocking in that time period—such techniques were not as common then).

He is saying, "Now what?"

And we have no answer for him.

GIVE ME YOUR FEEDBACK:
THE 400 BLOWS

1. Of all the activities young Antoine could enjoy in his forbidden outings, he goes to the cinema. Why does Truffaut have Antoine interested in film?

2. Antoine has some serious mental and behavioral issues, revealed both at school and at home. Name some of the scenes and events and note how they reveal the nature of his personal problems.

3. What do you expect will happen to Antoine now that he has reached his goal: getting to the sea?

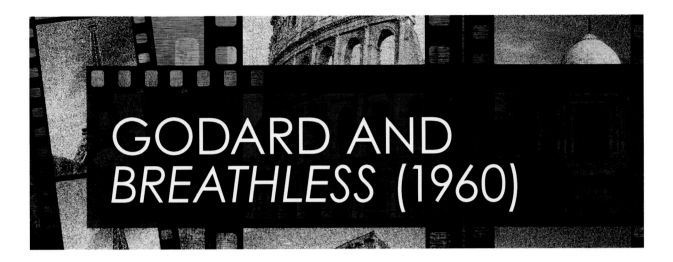

GODARD AND *BREATHLESS* (1960)

Imagine you were in a film production course. I was teaching you to actually make films: how to write a story, how to coach the actors, how to edit the footage together. The whole process. You are trying to learn how to tell a story visually, in a way your audience will understand it and hopefully care about what happens.

The first night of that class, I could very easily show you this film, Jean Luc Godard's *Breathless* (1960) and tell you, "This film does virtually everything wrong. As you make your own films, it is an example of everything to avoid doing!"

True, virtually every New Wave film breaks the rules of Hollywood filmmaking. But Godard really goes off the deep-end. His actors look directly into the camera and sometimes even talk to the film audience. His music almost never matches the mood of the scene. *And his editing?!!* It's absolutely shocking. I actually have students—good ones—who sincerely ask, "Does this guy really even know what he's doing?"

But what if he actually does? What if he knows the normal language of film and is deliberately playing around with it? Even mocking it—and our expectations as viewers! *That* becomes a more interesting question.

Jean Luc Godard was a young man who had seen more films (French, American, lots of stuff) than most filmmakers of his era would have seen. Indeed, the core group of young *cinephiles* who sat in the dark and watched hundreds of films had more film exposure than was perhaps even possible until the arrival of the videotape. Yet after all that, he chose, not to copy and follow after most of what he saw in normal commercial cinema. Instead, he was like a musician who doesn't just cover a popular song

as faithfully as possible, but plays around with it. Morphs it into something new. And in the process, makes it his own.

His first feature film *Breathless* is the story of a cheap crook. He runs afoul of the cops and decides to skip town. He's going to ask his girl to go with him, grab his loot and bail. Exactly like we see in hundreds of other crime films! But Godard doesn't just copy what they've all done before. He tips it on its head and keeps his audience guessing. He plays around with the way shots are supposed to be cut together in order to keep them logical. He lets the actors acknowledge the presence of the camera (and with it the audience) and even crack jokes with us. He breaks so many classic rules that you actually have to watch harder than usual. Our protagonist orders breakfast at a café and then leaves, never to get it. He fires a gun to his right, at a man approaching him from the left. He escapes the scene of a crime by running directly *toward* the event, not away from it.

And throughout the film, he uses the crime film slang, the gangster body language, dresses like Hollywood criminals. He clearly tries to pattern his life after Humphrey Bogart crime films.

So *Breathless* could serve as an object lesson on how *not* to make a movie. But it is also a very daring choice by a new director to go a completely different direction with a very tired and clichéd story. What we get is a great many more laughs than one might have expected for the time. A boat-full of reminders that what we are watching is a movie (and that the filmmaker and actors know it too). None of the characters is really very believable. Even the leading characters, who are clearly huge star-crossed lovers, don't seem to really love each other. There is a nonchalance, a feeling that they are going through the motions. And the end of the film is a pay-off of the contrived, even silly, sort of artificial relationship they have. Throughout, they are clearly more interested in themselves than in their lover. But it goes deeper than that. It is as if you are being invited to watch an actor play at being a character and what we see is the actor pretending to express the emotions that the character is supposed to be feeling.

As you watch other Godard films, his spirit will change. The amusing mockery of *Breathless* will be replaced by political statements, anger, and disgust. At one point, he will even portray our society as a mob of cannibals. Frankly, I, personally, do not care much for most of his films. However, he is without question one of the most important directors of the New Wave and even if he never made another film, I believe *Breathless* sets the cinematic stage for change. The film seems like a giant rift torn through the road. It's just that important.

GIVE ME YOUR FEEDBACK:
BREATHLESS

1. After viewing *Breathless* for yourself, do you believe Godard could have made it much more conventionally? Was he able to make a "normal" film—and is this a deliberate "mash up" if you will?

2. Does the way he edits the film, with jump cuts, missing pieces, jarring and confusing scenes, make you feel more interested in the characters and the story or less involved (as if you were being distanced by the director)?

3. The star of the film, Jean-Paul Belmondo, became a huge star after this film. What qualities in his performance do you see that would cause people to embrace him?

FIRST CINEMA—SECOND CINEMA—THIRD CINEMA

SOLANAS AND GETINO

In the late 1960s and early '70s, two Latin American film critics, Fernando Solanas and Octovio Gettno suggested a way of categorizing films.[28] They broke down cinema into types they simply called "first," "second" and "third" based on the primary intent of the film. According to these two men, "first cinema" was film as consumer product. The film's intent was to make money and the makers (especially in the Hollywood industry) knew that telling an entertaining story with characters we care about often appeal to an extremely large audience—and therefore make a lot of money. So first cinema is entertainment cinema. Money-making cinema. And these guys were staring right at Hollywood when they wrote about it!

Second cinema is primarily what we would most likely call "art cinema." The film is not made primarily in hopes of making massive amounts of money. It is a form of personal expression, almost as if the film screen is the director's canvas and he or she is a painter. The best-known examples of second cinema are the *auteur* filmmakers from the 1960s. We are meeting a few of them here: François Truffaut, Ingmar Bergman, Fellini. They used film to explore ideas that interested them personally. Cinema was their canvas. For viewers, the appeal is to explore the world sharing the eyes of that filmmaker. We may even meet with friends after the film and talk about our feelings toward the film. Some of us might even go on to become cinema majors in college, studying these films almost endlessly.

But Solanas and Getino were social and political activists. They wanted us to do more than just study and discuss films as an intellectual exercise. And they certainly didn't want viewers to just pay their money and be entertained! They wanted to encourage films to be a more active social force—an instrument that would struggle and confront and perhaps even change the world they came from. Specifically speaking to the film community in Latin America, they called for film to "join the cause," if you will. Expose corruption. Condemn injustice. Prosecute those whose evil was being ignored. Even be a weapon for widespread social change. In fact, their best-known essay called third cinema *a gun*. A weapon that fires 24 frames per second![29]

Solanas and Getino would have no interest in an intimate film about dreams or one man's personal search for God. They'd absolutely start a riot if their local theater showed a Hollywood entertainment film—whether it was *Some Like it Hot* or *Guardians of the Galaxy*, wouldn't matter to them.

EXPANDING THE CONCEPT

So Solanas and Getino called for Latin American cinema to be third cinema—attack cinema, if you will. I'd like to use their division of films, but to expand the concept a bit. Obviously we are all familiar with first cinema. I imagine anyone reading this book has seen more than their fair-share of entertainment films (perhaps not just American ones, but from places like France or Bollywood). Second cinema

---

[28] Fernando Solanas and Octavio Getino, "Towards a Third Cinema" in: *Movies and Methods. An Anthology*, ed. Bill Nichols. (Berkeley: University of California Press, 1976), 44–64.

[29] In cases you didn't know, the motion picture camera and projector run at 24 frames per second, so this is a direct comparison between the power of cinema and automatic weapons fire.

might be less familiar to some of us, but in this book we get at least a quick overview of some of the very best works of the type. Third cinema, however, might require a bit of reworking. The way I see it, third cinema is attack cinema. That would certainly include the most brazen film calling for revolution, but it doesn't necessarily have to go that direction. For our purposes here, a film that exposes corruption in a government, or even one that reveals that former Nazi officers have gone unpunished and are holding prestigious government positions and are living a life of luxury. To me, that is third cinema as well.

And it certainly isn't limited to Central and South America. It is a global film experience—based on primary *intent*.

One last but extremely important note: Although they sound similar never confuse "Third World Cinema" with "Third Cinema." Third cinema is a type of film and it is not limited to a particular part of the globe. It is absolutely possible for a director to make a film that is clearly an example of third cinema—criticizing a government, even calling for a revolution, anywhere in the world. That sort of film can even be made in America!

What follows is a small assortment of *second* cinema masterworks, clearly films that the director made as works of personal expression and a couple of *third cinema* pieces that confront evil in the society where the films were made. Those third cinema films may not qualify as what Solanas and Getino intended when they compared film with a gun, but in my mind, they are still excellent examples of socially aware films that accuse and attack in their own way.[30]

---

[30] The final film in this text, *3 Idiots*, is the exception. It is a Bollywood blockbuster, made to appeal to a large mass audience and make lots of money. But there's still interesting content just below the surface and I am confident you will find it an exceptional film well-worth our attention. I can hardly wait to share it with you!

FELLINI AND 8 ½ (1963)

FROM NEOREALIST TO AUTEUR

Federico Fellini began his film education in the Italian neorealism movement. He worked with some of the best-known names of the movement and even won an Academy Award for his screenplay of *Rome, Open City*. He would go on to both write and assistant direct another neorealist classic, *Paisan*. When that short-lived movement faded and Fellini began making his own films, many fans of neorealism were happy to think of this as a new chapter in that movement's history.

To those people, the film *8 ½* must have been quite a shock—and a great disappointment. Fellini completely "flew off the rails" making a film that was the exact opposite of a neorealist film. The film is totally internal—within the mind (and spirit) of the director himself. Dreams. Fantasy. A strange, floating quality, as if the characters were almost in some sort of choreographed dance. And above all, an absurd quality. You can say many things about neorealism, but words like "fantasy" and "absurd" are not going to appear!

To me, this transformation, this new philosophy, is when Fellini really comes into his own. *8 ½* is his masterwork, not a bizarre misstep. He cuts loose from the objective world portrayed by the neorealists and turns inward—his own mind becomes his playground. The mind operates in a much different way than a bombed out Italian city. The mind is about images and feelings, not plot. Tell me, when you awake from a nightmare, do you remember a complex story and how logical it all was? No—you were frightened by some particular image! How many of us who write a short story obsess over the accuracy of the externals and tell a story that is completely grounded in the real world, so much so, that the story could be a news report of an actual

incident? Yes, some of us do, but even those who write about a real place and real events often color that reality with the subjective perspective of the narrator, or imagine it how it *could* have happened if something were changed.

Or maybe as we write our "reality based" and "objective" story, we find ourselves describing just how the event made us *feel*.

This is Fellini breaking free. *8 ½* begins with a dream. A dream that doesn't even make sense. No, that's the wrong word! The dream is not a logical, story-driven experience. But does it "make *sense*"? That's exactly what it does. The filmmaker's dreams are all about senses: the sense of claustrophobia, the horrible choking, gasping feeling of being unable to breathe. The feeling of flying, but even here there are specific sensations created. This is not the joyous euphoria of happily flying across the clear blue sky. It's is terrifying. Something I am not supposed to be able to do. I am out of control!

All of this in just the first moments of the film. And it tells us so much. Before we even know what the man does, we know he the panic he feels, we know how out-of-control he feels. Of course it's not neorealism! The whole film is about feeling. It is about images in the mind, not intricate plots. Some critics spend huge amounts of time trying to establish what scenes in the film "really happen" and which are "just fantasy." Do you see how silly this seems? The protagonist of the film doesn't sit objectively looking down on events as if he is a god on Olympus. He sees through his own eyes—his own mind. In fact, that subjective state is all any of us ever get. And *8 ½* explores this subjective view of the world like few others in the history of cinema.

Fellini makes the protagonist of *8 ½* an alter-ego for himself—a film director. But Guido (Marcello Mastroianni in a masterful performance) is incapacitated by a terrible artistic block. I don't believe Fellini shares that same block. He seems more to have so much inspiration, *so much* he wants to express that the only way he is able to describe it is as a grand parade. A circus. He is the ringmaster and all the performers are the faces and feelings of his life. Get that? While he may set up his director protagonist as someone who cannot express himself—it is only a setup that allows for him to gradually reveal his own feelings, his own inspirations, and in the end he can no longer hold back his feelings and the circus comes to life.

Ultimately, Fellini's autobiographical character, Guido, envisions his life as a grand circus—and all the people he has known are performers. *8 ½* (1963).

The people of Guido's world are not real people. If we could somehow jump into the film and actually meet them as if they were real, we would have very different perspectives on them. And for Fellini, that's the point. He (or his alter ego) sees these people through his own eyes and heart—indeed the only way any of us see anybody! His memory of childhood, watching a prostitute walking by is seen through the eyes of a young boy. She is huge, exotic, threatening. Is his Ideal Woman (Claudia Cardinale) real or imagined? She is certainly real to him.

So I watch the climax of the film over and over, as Guido admits that he has failed and there will be no film. I see him duck under the table at his news conference and draw a gun from his pocket. I even hear a gunshot. And I ask myself over and over—was it real? Did he really commit suicide at the ill-fated press conference? Was it a fantasy? Perhaps some film critic who is much wiser than I will smile and tell me (patronizingly) that there's a clear answer and that I should think it's obvious. Honestly, I don't believe it really matters. The whole film is about the fantasy, the subjective, the feelings. What matters is that with his death (real or imagined) and the admission that there is no film, Guido's spirit is freed. His writer's block is gone and Fellini's own inspiration is allowed to come gushing out.

In a circus.

GIVE ME YOUR FEEDBACK:
8 ½

1. Having seen the ending of the film, do you personally believe Guido actually shot himself or is this just a fantasy?

2. Religious figures, such as priests, often appear in the film. What role does religion—and feelings of guilt—play in Guido's creative block?

3. What does *auteur* mean? Why is Fellini used as a prime example of an auteur director?

Chapter 20

INGMAR BERGMAN'S
THE SEVENTH SEAL (1957)

"I want God to put out His hand, show His face, speak to me.

I cry out to Him in the dark but there is no one there."

—The Knight, *The Seventh Seal*

Much as we saw with Federico Fellini, Ingmar Bergman is an auteur director who uses film as his canvas, painting on it his personal questions and feelings. Perhaps that's where the similarities end. While Fellini was the ringmaster of some absurdist circus, Bergman was a somber student of the human experience. The films from the middle of his career intently explored Man's relationship to God. They asked questions about the meaning of humanity's existence. In his old age, Bergman's films turn to explore memory and we see a mature soul trying to find meaning for his life in the memories he has accumulated over his lifetime.

A little voice in my head protests, "There's no way this guy should have been a filmmaker!" In a way that's true. This is certainly not the sort of subject we'd expect from most filmmakers. No wonder a film like *The Seventh Seal* is not particularly popular, even among film authorities, even today. It's so stylized. So visual—not verbal. It's almost like viewing a Byzantine painting. I can recognize the figures, but they are presented in a manner I find to be very … foreign. Even if the film I am viewing is full of comic book super heroes, it's still based on an external logic. In comparison, this film is so stark,

so existential. As famed film critic Roger Ebert said, "Films are no longer concerned with the silence of God but with the chattering of men."[31]

THE PLOT

The Seventh Seal tells of a knight returning home after the Crusades. He finds his homeland devastated by plague and the doom he sees around him only reflects the spiritual darkness he feels in his heart. He is hopeless. While he is traveling determinately toward his wife and home, he never seems eager to reach them. Even before he meets Death, do you feel like he's on his last journey—and he knows it?

And the knight meets Death. Yes, Death. Not some joke or a parody or a cliché. The spirit world is incorporated into the world of *The Seventh Seal* just as stark and direct as the waves we see crashing against the jagged black rocks. The knight challenges Death to a game of chess. Think about it. The only way a filmmaker would dare do something like this is as comedy. Not Bergman. He plays it deadly straight (excuse the pun)—and it works.

The chess match goes on for most of the film and it's the element of *The Seventh Seal* that draws my attention time and time again. If the knight knows he cannot win, why play at all? Like so many of the films from the world of second cinema, the meaning is left to each individual viewer. But for me, it's a delaying tactic. The knight cannot win, but as long as the game goes on, he is not taken and is allowed to finish his journey.

---

[31] Roger Ebert, "The Seventh Seal." *Great Movie*. Ebert On-Line.com. April 16, 2000.

Ingmar Bergman's *The Seventh Seal* (1957)   77

And just perhaps, this final journey will provide him some sort of illumination. Some sort of whisper from a God he cannot find.

So the game is on and the stakes are life and death. I think we learn a great deal about what kind of person this knight is, by watching the game. He is not afraid. In fact, he displays a will of cold steel playing the game at all. He's been in life and death games before and they don't scare him. I think he is even fascinated by his unique opportunity to glimpse this legendary spiritual creature up close. This man is never shown doing anything heroic. He's never shown fighting a horde of villains, but he can look Death himself right in the eye without blinking.

As long as the game continues, the bleak journey can continue. The knight encounters various people. He sees the ravages of the Black Death throughout the land. He plays on. He travels on. He continues asking for God to reveal Himself at last. And he hears nothing.

In the end, does the knight ever hear from God? Does he ever really have his faith rewarded and renewed? Again, the auteur leaves the true meaning to you and me individually. But the thing that stands out to me is not what this man learns about God, but what he learns about himself.

THE SECRET VICTORY

Perhaps you believed that somehow reaching home would bring safety. Perhaps you believed seeing his wife would somehow soothe the knight's broken soul. The visit to his castle is extremely anticlimactic. There is a brief embrace with the wife he has not seen in years, but there is no relief here. Once we finally reach it, the castle proves to be just a house—not home.

It isn't the illumination he searched for, but along the journey, the knight does indeed gain an idea. The chess match gains new significance. Indeed, it gains a level of meaning that even Death does not see. As checkmate comes ever closer and as both players see its ominous approach, the knight makes one last move. It isn't so much the move of a piece on the board as it is a final gambit in life. One last battle. The difference is that this time, no one knows about it but him. The game consumes Death (and his anticipation of finally collecting the knight) and *he misses something*. I am torn in how to write this because if you have not seen the film, I do not want to spoil the most meaningful moments of the film for you. However, I want to make it clear. The knight plays a game Death doesn't even see. The stakes are still life and death, but this time, it's not the knight's life.

So in the end, the knight loses the chess game, but when Death looks in those cold steel eyes and sees just the hint of a smile on the knight's face, he has no idea what has just happened. And the knight will literally go to his grave and never tell a soul that he won his last battle.

And so *The Seventh Seal* ends, almost like a silent film from decades earlier. Without words. With a striking image that only one man is able to see.

The Dance of Death begins. Perhaps now, the knight will have his questions answered at last.

GIVE ME YOUR FEEDBACK:
THE SEVENTH SEAL

1. Who do the traveling acrobat, his wife, and their baby represent and what does this mean to the knight?

2. In contrast to the serious, pious knight, what sort of person is his squire?

3. Have you ever personally seen another film that made a *serious* examination of the relationship between God and Man?

THE MARRIAGE OF MARIA BRAUN (1979)

"What doesn't kill makes me stronger."

—Friedrich Nietzsche

"Nietzsche died insane."

—Bob Jordan

NEW GERMAN CINEMA

To my mind, one of the most interesting things about the European *auteur* directors is how unique and different each one is. The artist/directors of West Germany have that same unique quality, but they also share an important link. They are a part of something that became known as **New German Cinema**. This movement was made up of young filmmakers who looked at German cinema after World War II and saw two obvious problems. First, Germany's Nazi past and specifically the Holocaust were practically like family secrets you kept in the closet and never examined—certainly not the sort of thing you'd air in public! Today, many of us might think of World War II as being only something you read about in history books, but for Germans in the 1950s and '60s, it was their daily life just a few years before. Second, in the post-war period, Germany had basically been rebuilt in the American image. In fact, a West German of that period might now be blamed if he felt like his native country didn't exist anymore.

Rather than deny these issues, the new generation of West German filmmakers confronted both of them—in some rather innovative and daring ways. Volker Schlöndorff can present a film like *Young*

Törless (1966) about boys in military school who descend into violence, sadism and a very twisted sort of homoeroticism, which is clearly intended to evoke Nazism.[32] New German Cinema also brings us the films of **Wim Wenders**, who seems to always present characters who are alienated, lonely, and homeless. In *Wings of Desire* (1987), we see angels who are lonely and feel separated from the world they are sentenced to watch trod by. *Alice in the Cities* (1974) tells the story of a young man who accidentally becomes the caregiver for a young girl, Alice. They begin a long, hopeless search for Alice's grandmother—without knowing her name or where she lives. It's as if they are lost in an unfamiliar land that is no longer Germany.

R. W. FASSBINDER: "ENFANT TERRIBLE"

Fassbinder was really *wacked*. I believe that's the correct academic term for it. He was notorious for abusing massive amounts of drugs. His violent sexual urges are the stuff of tabloid legend. He forced his secretary to become an actress and then cast in her in nothing but degrading roles. Off screen, she claimed he once beat her almost to death in the middle of the street. Lovers who abused him. Others whom he abused. It was a massive drug overdose that killed him, at 37, and left the world wondering what other films he might have made. Film historians usually have difficulty identifying start dates and end dates for major cinematic movements. There is no debate on this one. The death of Fassbinder is considered to be the end of New German Cinema.

---

[32] And which will also bring to mind *Lord of the Flies*, obviously.

Wild, self-destructive libertine? Of course. But he was also one of the most prolific directors you are likely to study. In a career that lasted less than 15 years, he completed 40 feature length films; two television series, several short productions and more than 20 stage plays. Given his frenzied production pace, you might believe his films would appear crude and rushed. On the contrary, many look polished, even elegant. The cinematography of a film like *The Marriage of Maria Braun* or *World on a Wire* (1973) is simply breathtaking. (Significantly both are the work of cinematographer Michael Ballhaus.) His are some of the most elegant domestic melodramas you will ever see, but they are packed so full of twists and quirky characters, they are never really what you expect.

And he was a genius—no one will debate that. Fassbinder was fascinated by society's outcasts—the people who have fallen through the cracks. His films somehow weave together the horrors of Germany's Nazi past, the alienation and loneliness of modern life and the pain forever felt by the losers of the world. The images on the screen are beautiful. The people and the world they live in are not.

THE MARRIAGE OF MARIA BRAUN (1979)

I suppose on paper *The Marriage of Maria Braun* is a pretty simple story: After a chaotic wedding during a World War II bombing, Maria loses her husband in a far-off battle and spends much of the movie trying to find him. Once he returns, he confesses to a murder Maria committed and goes to prison. Maria spends the rest of the film trying to get ahead so she is prepared when her husband finally comes home.

You know what that sounds like? A domestic melodrama from the late 1940s. That may be the plot and that may be the genre, but it isn't even close to what we experience with the movie, is it!

Perhaps the most important thing I can say to anyone studying this film is that *Maria is Germany*. During the war, she is struggling to survive. She gathers scraps of wood and bits of food, wherever they could be found. Time goes by, the war ends, but the Allied soldiers are still there. She essentially hustles them. She works at a seedy café, dancing with the lonely soldiers. All the while, she searches for her husband, even though everyone believes him to be dead.

Again, I am torn. Do I assume you have seen the film or do I try to avoid spoilers? The return of Maria's husband is one of the funniest and most bizarre moments in the film. It also leads directly to what is essentially the second half of the film—Herr Braun is in prison (for a crime committed by his wife) and Maria does just what she does so well—survives and gets ahead. Now she even finds money and success in the amazing place that is the new Germany.

It's so twisted. That's what we're supposed to do, isn't it? We survive the bad times. We do what we need to do in order to get ahead. We rise is stature and earn money. That's the happy ending. That's the American dream, isn't it?

Isn't it?

Not the way Fassbinder sees it. Maria's broken somewhere along the line—broken inside. I think she's lost her soul. She is a survivor. She is brilliant. She is always up front with people, even when it's to tell them she is there to torment and destroy them. I'd call her a narcissist or a psychopath or something, but those sorts of people are absorbed with themselves. Maria doesn't even care about herself. She cares about one thing in the whole film: getting her husband back. Nothing else matters. And in the process of achieving that goal, she destroys everything around her—even herself.

Someday I hope I can do a detailed psychological study of Maria Braun. I think it would be extremely interesting. The way she takes joy in making her receptionist cry. The way she utterly crushes her lover (and boss) Herr Oswald and describes it to him even as she does it.

The ending? People argue about this film's conclusion even today. Is it some sort of deliberate act—a conclusion for Maria because now that her husband is back, there is nothing left? Is it some twisted accident that a mad director forced onto the story? Two things I can say here—first, that the soccer game (excuse me, football) drowning out the story of the film adds to the absurdity of the climax; second, that no matter what causes the "events" at the end of the film, Maria is tired and has no more reason to live.

The actress Hanna Schylugga *owns* this film. Maria Braun is one of the most cold, inhuman monsters you are like to ever see on the screen. And so fascinating that you cannot take your eyes off of her.

And remember, to Fassbinder, *Maria is Germany.*

GIVE ME YOUR FEEDBACK:
THE MARRIAGE OF MARIA BRAUN

1. Okay, here's my main question. Do you feel like Maria's "act" at the end of the film is deliberate or accidental?

2. List three events in the film that tell you something important about Maria's personality.

3. It is often said that Fassbinder's kind, meek characters are the ones most often destroyed. Are there any examples of this in *Maria Braun*? What does this tendency in his films tell us about the man himself?

THE OFFICIAL STORY (1985)

This is Third Cinema (not to be confused with third world cinema, remember). It isn't primarily an entertainment product made to reach a large mass audience and make lots of money. It is not a personal, subjective work of artistic expression meant to serve as an *auteur* director's canvas. It is meant to attack. It is meant to expose and criticize social injustice. I would not compare it with a gun, as Solanas and Getino describe, but it's at least a prosecutor.

From the perspective of someone studying cinema, however, I personally find that most works of Third Cinema do not age very well. The injustice they attack becomes ancient history and the specific historical events fade from mind. Perhaps this is best. Maybe the fact that a brutal regime ends and the films exposing it become dated is a good thing. Of course, then I remember that when one injustice ends, it is only replaced by others. It will never end.

Wow, I got depressed, just then! Back to the Third Cinema. *The Official Story* is a wonderful, cutting film that might not be a call to take up guns in the street, but it at least strips away layers of obfuscation and denial and shows a very secret, dirty war. Today as the years crawl away, it might not be as well-known as the latest social injustice, but it's hard to forget thousands of Argentine women in the plaza marching with huge posters of their missing children asking the government, "Where have you taken them?" And the film was made perhaps three years after that very government ran off and tried to hide in the dark corners like rats.

I think the thing that catches my attention most powerfully is that our protagonist is herself a history professor. But she is a history professor who is shockingly blind to the current history that is happening all around her in her daily life. She is deliberately ignorant to her own society (with good cause, as we shall see). The film has all the hallmarks of a political thriller (in the very best sense), but it keeps reminding us that it is based on too-real events. It keeps us uncomfortable in a way *Three Days of the Condor* just doesn't manage.

Our protagonist, Alicia is played by Norma Aleandro, who had been a South American film icon—a true movie star, when she was forced to leave her own country in the 1970s because her progressive political views upset the military government. She could not return to Argentina until the military junta fell in 1982. Two years later, she found herself playing a wife and mother, in full denial of the actions of her husband and the government he embraced. Alicia's whole life was based on blindness and lies. This is what I mean about the film staying uncomfortable and raw for the viewer. For the people making this film, they were creating people *they actually knew.* They may have been making a movie, but it portrayed the fight through their own reality from just months earlier.

We see Alicia teaching at a boys' school, keeping the focus of her modern Argentinian history class comfortably rooted on safe topics from decades earlier and confidently silencing anyone who brings up the current state of things. At home, we see that she's a devoted wife and mother. Indeed, her whole life seems to revolve around her charming daughter, Gaby. It's Gaby's fifth birthday and Alicia's mind naturally returns to a road she's clearly traveled before—Who are Gaby's birth parents? What happened to them? So yes, Gaby was adopted. But what catches your attention is that Alicia's husband, Roberto, a government official, resents the questions and insists that his wife not ask them. Roberto begins to go from an affectionate father to a suspicious figure with secrets that quickly start to bother the viewer—and Alicia. I simply love the way this film makes the audience feel we are watching only the most recent events in a very real family that has existed for years—had these sorts of conversations for years. But for some reason, this time, Alicia cannot let go. Maybe it's the girl's birthday. Maybe the shouting in the streets is becoming too loud to ignore, even inside this safe, comfortable home.

While it's difficult to turn our eyes away from Alicia, her husband Roberto (Hector Alterio) is equally fascinating. We are catching him in the middle of a transformation. His whole world is falling apart around him and we are watching every terrifying moment of it. He chose a side in the battle. Maybe it wasn't all at once. Maybe it was as much ignorance as it was greed or arrogance, but nonetheless, he made a choice. His choice brought a pretty house. It brought washing machines and nice clothes, but now the bill has come due. You can feel Roberto's fear rising. It's palpable. Work may be in a bright, air-conditioned high rise, but rats are scurrying everywhere, abandoning a sinking ship. And Roberto was too blind or too stupid or arrogant—whatever it was—he didn't get out in time. Now, day by day, he is losing it. Literally going insane from the fear. Early in the film, he is reintroduced to his wife's friend, Ana. He's confident enough to condemn her as being part of the problem that he helped try to destroy. Later, when he meets Sara, the woman Alicia believes just might be Gaby's grandmother, he totally loses control. The fear has taken hold and this "Mother from the Plaza" and all her uncomfortable questions have actually invaded his home!

I wish to backtrack here for a moment. Alicia's dear school friend Ana, comes for a visit. They sing the old school songs, eat and drink and have all those wonderful feelings we all get when we are reunited with a chum not seen in years. But with the late hour and the alcohol, Ana gradually begins to relax and

her lifelong friend asks her a question you know she's been asked before. "Why did you leave?"

But this time, she answers.

It's a wonderful scene. If I were a drama student, I'd be figuring out how to do it for a class project. The dear friends continue to laugh, continue to drink. And Ana opens up and begins, casually at first, to describe what happened. She was a victim of the Dirty War, herself. She was a disappeared one, just like the ones those people the women in the plaza shout about. Somehow she survived and came back. *But not all of her made it.*

"Why did you leave?" Such a simple question. Such a painful answer. Alicia finally comes to truly understand her dearest friend. *The Official Story* (1985).

So Alicia the history teacher gets a lesson in current history. A cruel one. I think the violence of the film's climax is made even more painful by the viewer's feelings that we are seeing real people. Alicia's eyes are torn open for the very first time. The thing she loves most in the world is what's at risk for her. Roberto is a man who made a deal with the devil and has lost everything—his family, his life, his soul.

Is this what Solanas and Getino meant when they called film a gun that fires at 24 frames per second? No.

It's a knife in your heart.

GIVE ME YOUR FEEDBACK:
THE OFFICIAL STORY

1. When do you first realize that Roberto is a part of a corrupt and evil government?

2. Why does Roberto react so strongly to the appearance of this older woman, Sara, being invited into his house?

3. Roberto takes his wife and child to visit his family in the country, but they clearly don't visit there much. Why is there such tension in this visit?

MOOLAADÉ (2004)

If you sat and watched a few minutes of the Ousmane Sembène film, *Moolaadé*, you would probably have feelings of peace and simplicity, when thinking of the beautiful native African village that is our setting. This couldn't possibly be the sort of film Solanas and Getino would call Third Cinema, right?

Well, to your credit, I don't think they had this in mind either. But hear me out: this is a very quiet and gentle film, especially at the beginning, but it is about the tradition of female genital mutilation common throughout many countries in Africa. Ultimately, it grows into a very powerful fight between genders and cultural traditions. Indeed, it is gentle, but it is also an amazing clash between the old and the new.

Even the most-brief description grabs our attention (as well as creates sudden discomfort): In an obscure African village, young girls are forced to go through female genital mutilation (FGM) in an age-old tradition called "purification." With the lives of four little girls at stake, one mother stands up to "purification" with a tradition of her own—one that is just as ancient and revered, but diametrically opposed to it.

MOOLAADÉ

The tradition of *moolaadé* is similar to what in the West might be called "sanctuary" or "asylum." If someone requests your hospitality and protection, once given, you are solemnly obligated to keep your word and protect them. To betray moolaadé would be a horribly evil act.

In *Moolaadé*, two ancient and powerful traditions are at war. One mother sets a symbolic cord across the doorway—indicating that the children here are protected. Beyond that cord, they will be mutilated and perhaps even killed. *And so it begins.*

New Yorker Films/Photofest

So one mother goes against her village's unwavering adherence to "purification." Second wife, Collé, also honors an important tradition, but she has set in motion something she can't possibly imagine. A rift is created between men and women, between modern ways and ancient tradition. The director of the film may use an extremely quiet and gentle approach, but the subject is one of the most disturbing and contemporary subjects mentioned anywhere in this book.

Ousmane Sembène was called "The Father of African Cinema." His place in film history is almost unique. Some directors (India's Satyajit Ray comes to mind) can claim to be the first, or in some cases, only filmmaker from their country recognized and appreciated internationally. Sembène has been the single director from the *entire continent* who has been recognized and appreciated globally.[33] He had a 40 year film career (and a career as an author that spanned roughly 50 years) and covered such topics as slavery, European colonialization of Africa and the spread of Islam across the continent. He had a gentle style, but used it to confront hard issues. I would compare him with Mahatma Gandhi.

So in one unnoticed African village, a revolution is starting. The village elders (male) and the purifiers (horrifying women in red, brandishing their circumcision knives) confront Collé, who stands alone. Gradually, the stakes grow. Women are forbidden radios (their one form of exposure to the outside world). A young man from the village returns home after school in France and finds himself in the middle of this tug of war. A traveling salesman tries to stay out of the fray, but in the end has to take sides. Eventually, all the women of the village decide where they will stand as well.

Sembène shows a remarkable level of understanding for his fellow native African people in this story. There is no "superior white Westerner" coming to this "backward" village to show them the "right way." Collé is a smart person who thinks through what is most important to her (protecting the children), develops a strategy to accomplish her goal and bravely follows through with her commitment, even if it hurts (terribly). I want to make it clear, I am in no way trying to be patronizing in the way that I made that statement. I placed the quotes around terms that might be made into clichés in many films—but Sembène doesn't work that way. He could have made his film characters all speak French—he had them speak a variety of African dialects. For Sembène, Europe wasn't any better, or smarter, than Africa.

I'd like to stop and spend a moment on the traveling salesman, a cynical womanizer called "Mercenary." He is a good example of Sembéne's approach. Despite the fact that he rips off his customers and fools around with the women of the village, we still like him (indeed, most of the village seems to like him as well). He remains neutral through much of the conflict—it's essential to his continued business. But somewhere along the line, we begin to see *why* he is nicknamed Mercenary. While the name would seem to indicate that he never takes sides, it actually came to him (indirectly) because he was the one who stood up to injustice and spoke up—when all his comrades kept their mouths shut. As you watch the film, keep an eye on this character. Some of what he does is obvious, but parts are much more subtle. And (without giving anything away) his fate in the end is never shown—another character *tells* us what happened. That's not the way you're supposed to make a film! Sembéne turns the gaze of the camera away from some of the most powerful moments of his story.

Female Genital Mutilation is outlawed in most countries, but the laws are not enforced and in parts of Africa, 90 percent of the women have been "cut." It is difficult to get many to talk about it, much less gather accurate statistics about it. From what I've read, something like 15 percent of the girls who undergo FGM die or have serious health issues. But my goal here not to analyze the practice, but to turn our attention, however briefly, to a single film that takes a giant social issue and turns it into a very small, but powerful story.

Even though a wide variety of critics have condemned the story film and its endearing characters, *Moolaadé* is an example of using just those characteristics to move the audience to understand an injustice. The film could be shown in China or Brazil or in Oklahoma and we would all understand it. We'd all feel for Collé and respect her strength. Solanas and Getino would adore this film, I am sure.

And in the end the old ostrich egg that has been sitting atop the temple for a hundred years is replaced by a television antenna.

---

[33] As with any such claim, there are of course a variety of complications. There are people who would insist on referring to him as "The Father of *Sub-Saharan* African Film." Others would include European ethnographic filmmakers like Jean Rouch. But I stand by the claim.

GIVE ME YOUR FEEDBACK:
MOOLAADÉ

1. What happens to the salesman, Mercenary? As viewers, how do we learn of this?

2. Why does the director frequently show us the pile of confiscated radios in ways that show us the village temple, the women doing chores and the men who are angry at the women's behavior?

3. Who sides with Collé (the second wife) at the beginning of the film and who is with her by the end?

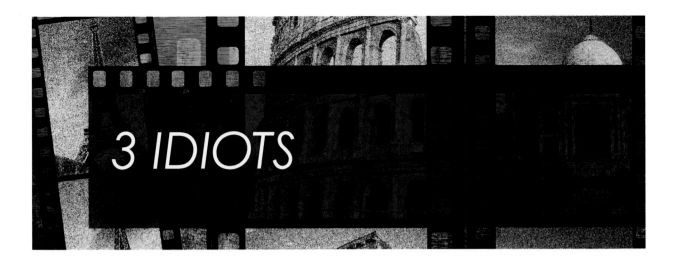

3 IDIOTS

"Just give us one star, six musical numbers, and three dance numbers. That's Bollywood!"

—Anonymous

A title can be so misleading. *3 Idiots* (2009). It sounds like we are about to watch a film like *Animal House* or *Porky's*. On some level this is sort of accurate. This will be a "going to college" film, be full of pranks and fun relationships. Even the predictable device of pitting the students against a tyrannical faculty member is right where you'd expect it. Add to the assumptions and clichés—this is a Bollywood film, an Indian entertainment film (Hindi specifically) in one of the largest industries in the world. Clearly, we would identify it as First Cinema—and I will note a couple of similarities and differences with Hollywood films of this sort.

I am no expert on Bollywood films, but the thing that becomes quickly apparent to the Westerner is that the typical Bollywood film includes elements of many different genres. An Indian audience considers this to be getting their money's worth! For example, you can see a film about military experts going under cover in a school in order to fight-terrorists, but still see musical numbers along with the bombs and gunplay (*Main Hoon Na*, 2004). A classic called *Sholay* (1975) has enough of a Western vibe that it spawned the nickname "Curry Western," similar to the Spaghetti Westerns of the 1960s. In contrast, an American film will limit itself to specific genre categories. You are unlikely to see Bruce Willis battling terrorists and have the supporting cast break into song and dance between the fights!

So it comes as no surprise that *3 Idiots* conforms with its Indian siblings. We have here a college comedy. And yes, there are musical numbers. And more than anything else, we have a story that is meant to entertain and characters we are supposed to care about. To me that is one of the most wonderful qualities about the film. It might be clichéd. There are corny moments that just don't work for the Western viewer. But despite it all, I come to care a great deal for these people— especially after viewing other foreign films that pride themselves on alienating the audience. Creating characters we are *not* meant to like. Plot situations that we are *supposed* to resist and disbelieve. It just seems refreshing to me to return to a film that presents us with people we empathize with and root for.

This film has a great deal going for it. It comes as no shock that it is one of the most successful Indian films in history. But what is most significant about *3 Idiots* (at least for me), is that it carries a very timely and sincere message about the society that made it. Beneath the camp and the silly college jokes, there is a rather pointed accusation about modern Indian society. The sort of testing that can determine what school a child attends, indeed the entire educational system is merely the old *caste system* (social class system), which will lock multiple generations into a particular niche. Some will be successful. Others will be locked into a lower or middle class, all thanks to a batch of academic tests and what school a person gets to attend. Even the student's parents or grandparents will be affected by the results of these high-pressure challenges. *3 Idiots* even addresses the suicide of several students due to the stress and importance of testing done by the existing education system.

A rebel hero. A young protagonist fighting the system. It isn't like we have never seen this before. I suppose this is *Footloose*. It's certainly *The 400 Blows* (a highly respected intellectual film if there ever was one). In *3 Idiots* we meet Rancho (one of India's biggest stars, Aamir Khan) who is to engineering what Mozart was to music. His genius and quick-on-his-feet thinking endear him to many of his classmates and just as quickly set him as a target for the school dean, nicknamed "Virus" (legendary character actor Boman Irani). But even while we laugh at his mischievous victories over the system, we are also beginning to see what is at the core of Rancho's fighting spirit—he hates the entire country's education/career-based caste system and wants to break free from it. And he wants to take with him anyone willing to follow him.

The essays in this book focus upon a variety of elements. Some of the films discussed in this book are noteworthy for their visual design. Others have remarkable performances by actors. Sometimes the film is most important when considered in its historical context. *3 Idiots* is interesting on two levels, in my opinion. First is the structure of the story. We watch two young men get word that a mysterious man called "Silencer" is coming to town. They drop everything—literally. One man, Farhan, escapes from a plane—even though it's already taken off. And his friend, Raju, has no pants. *Yes, he has no pants.* They meet Silencer and we discover he is a former school mate of theirs and that he considers them to be his mortal enemies. Farhan then tells us their story in flashback. To me, the flashback mode makes the story about memory and perspective over 10 years that have passed. Two buddies remember (and were influenced by) their college experiences. Their lives were literally transformed by an old friend.

Silencer's return has reignited the two friends' memories of school and their desire to find the absent member of their trio, Rancho. We are even given musical cues that express how they feel about him.

The main theme song is about a precious friend, how he was lost, and how we must now try to find him.

Like parallel train tracks, we switch back and forth between the current story of the search for Rancho and the story of the school days that affected each of them so deeply. There are some unexpected twists in each road, but ultimately, I don't believe there is much question about where either tale will end. However, we are so emotionally bound up with the characters, does it really matter?

The other facet of the film worth our attention here is the underlying social critique. I am neither well-traveled nor am I well-read on foreign cultures, so this film exposed me to something unfamiliar—perhaps it did this for you as well. Rancho and his friends are trapped. Enslaved in a caste system, just as surely as their great-grandparents. This class system is built on educational success and career success. As one of the characters in the film says, "No education. No career. No beautiful home. No pretty wife!" Along with the fart jokes and the corny musical numbers, we are learning something. The extreme pressure for students is so intense here that youth suicide has skyrocketed. An entire family's future rides on the student's performance, almost as if the child were a prized race horse everyone has bet upon. *Bet everything.*

So there are transformations of several characters here. Two friends, terrified and trapped on the treadmill, learn to be the men they really want to be. Even Silencer changes. He becomes obsessed with winning the horrible race that is shown destroying his classmates. And Rancho changes too. Maybe not for himself, but for us as viewers, most certainly. Our perception of him changes from class clown to, well, messiah. He preaches against the system and offers a different way.

So perhaps, I am making too much of a simple Bollywood entertainment film. But I don't think so. Hopefully, when you see it, you will know what I mean.

EPILOGUE

*May we meet someday in the gardens of Daisen-in,
where we will sit beside the laughing waterfall and
cool our feet in her crystal streams.*